Special

Activities

For

Grandparents and Grandchildren

Jana Dube Hletko

and

Lynn Zacny Busby

Third Guidebook in a Series About
Spending Special Time
With Grandchildren

Copyright 2019 by Jana Dube Hletko

All rights reserved. No part of this book may be used or reproduced by any means, graphic, electronic, or mechanical, including photocopying, recording, taping or by any information storage retrieval system without the written permission of the publisher except in the case of brief quotations embodied in critical articles and reviews.

ISBN-13:
9781794063891

Cover Illustration by Lynn Alpert.
Photography by Jana Dube Hletko and Lynn Zacny Busby and others as noted.
Permission obtained for pictures by Elizabeth Antias and Patrick Bowden 1/12/2019.

Notice: Any products or company names used throughout the book have not been solicited. Neither Jana nor Lynn has received any compensation for their use.

Notice: Every effort has been made to locate the copyright owners of any material used in this book. Please let us know of any error, and we will gladly make any necessary corrections in subsequent printings.

Other Books by Jana D. Hletko and Lynn Zacny Busby:

Cousins Camp	Cousins Camp 2.0: A Grandparents Guide to Spending Special Time with Grandchildren	100 Plus Things To Do With Your Grandchildren
A Guide to Spending Special Time with Your Grandchildren	An update of the original Cousins Camp Book	A How-To Guide For Grandparents, By Grandparents

Table of Contents

Introduction _____ 6

INDOORS _____ 8

In The Kitchen _____ 8

Enroll in a Cooking Subscription Service _____ 8
Make Rainbow Colored Ice Cubes _____ 9
Decorate a Fun Cake _____ 10
Make Buckeyes or Buckeye Fudge _____ 11
Halloween Hot Dog Mummies _____ 13
Meatloaf Foot _____ 15
Vomiting Pumpkin _____ 16
   Easy Guacamole dip _____ 16
Candy Corn Jello _____ 17
Easter Bunny Cake _____ 18
April Fools Dessert Sliders _____ 20
Cinnamon Applesauce Ornaments _____ 21
Valentine's Day Cookie Pizza _____ 23
Turkey Cupcakes _____ 24

In The Craft Room _____ 25

Create Your Own Picture Book _____ 25
Make a Scrapbook of a Parent Growing Up _____ 26
Make a Keepsake Book of Cards _____ 27
Create Art with Raised Salt Painting _____ 28
Create Art String Painting or Pulled String Art _____ 29
Make Perler Bead Bowls _____ 31
Make Paper Snowflakes _____ 32
Make Multi-Colored Coffee Filter Bowls _____ 33
Create Tissue Paper Stained Glass _____ 34
Experiment with More Stained Glass Projects _____ 36
Make Sea Glass Vases _____ 37
Make Paper Corner Bookmarks _____ 38
Make Fingerprint Art Glass Magnets _____ 39
Make Decorative Clipboards _____ 41
Have Fun with Fleece _____ 43
   Make a No Sew Fleece Scarf _____ 43
   Make A No-Sew Pet Pillow Cover _____ 45

Make Fabric Wall "Art"_____47
Make Sun Melted Crayons _____48
   Use Sun-Melted Crayons Art Activity _____49
Make a Leaf Rubbing _____50

*In The Game Room*_____*52*

Make a Fort _____52
Send a Postcard_____52
Start a Tradition _____54
   Take a recurring picture _____54
   Buy A Special Ornament Every Year _____55
Play Picture This _____56
Draw Partner Pictures _____56
Play Individualized Bingo_____57
Play Candy Ball - Saran Wrap Version _____58
Play Heads or Tails _____59
Play Twizzler Knot _____59
Work on a Crossword Puzzle Together_____60
Create a Family Tree or Website _____61
Play Cards_____63
   Panic_____64
   Slap Jack _____66
   Spoons _____68
   War _____69
Play Dice Games _____70
   Drop Dead _____70
   Pig_____72
Play the Candy Bar Game _____72

OUTDOORS (YARD/GARDEN/PARK) _____75

Have a Scavenger Hunt _____75
Have a Selfie Scavenger Hunt_____77
Have a Balloon or Beach Ball Race _____79
Play Feed a Cousin _____79
Go for a Detective's Walk _____80
Perform Random Acts of Kindness_____80
Go Horseback Riding (or Sponsor Lessons) _____82
Hold a Community Bike Wash_____84
Do Some Gardening Together _____85

Build a Little Free Library ___86
Play Frisbee Golf___87

ON THE GO ___89

Visit Your Grandchild's Home ___89
Attend a Seasonal Festival or Special Event___89
Visit an Ethnic Neighborhood ___94
Visit an Airport ___95
Rent a Motel/Hotel Room; Swim for the Day ___96
Attend a Special Event at a Zoo, Museum, or Garden___97
Go See the Synchronous Fireflies ___103
Take a Boat Ride/Shelling Excursion___105
Use Technology to Communicate With Grandchildren _106
   Use Text Messaging ___107
   Share Photos___108
   Use Video Conferencing (e.g. SKYPE)___109
   Read A Book Together Long-Distance Style___110
   Directions for Using Videoconferencing___110
   Use Old Fashioned Email ___111
   Use Facebook (Social Media)___111
   Create a Family Only Facebook Group ___114
   Add a Family Event on Facebook ___116
   Use Facebook to Discover Events Around You ___117
   Follow Your Grandchildren on Instagram ___118
Get To Know Internet Shortcuts the Kids Use ___119
   Get Creative With Emojis___119
   Try Using Some Texting Abbreviations ___120

Sometimes Things Won't Work As Planned __121
About the Authors ___122

Introduction

As we begin our third book filled with ideas on how to spend special time with your grandchildren, we are reminded how important this family time can be. There is no bond like the one between grandparents and their grandchildren. While that bond can take different forms... grandparents actually serving as parents, grandparents who live close by, grandparents who work on their relationships from a distance... it is a special one indeed.

The first book we collaborated on was *Cousins Camp*. It describes how to organize and live through a 5-7 day experience without parents involved and how to expand "camp" to include parents as well. It is a guide for long-distance grandparents who can host a camp for several days at one time though some of the ideas are still appropriate for shorter time spans. *Cousins Camp 2.0: A Grandparents Guide to Spending Special Time with Your Grandchildren* is an updated version of the same book, with expanded ideas and lists.

The second book, *101 Things To Do With Grandchildren*, gives grandparents lots of ideas for things to do whether they have a few hours or a few days. There are activities for museums, crafts, games, indoor and outdoor fun.

This book is organized in the same way: Activities are divided into INDOORS (kitchen, craft room, game room), OUTDOORS (pool/beach, yard/garden/ games), ON THE GO (an afternoon out/a field trip, an overnight excursion). Most of the activities are appropriate for children ages 4-12, but you will find that many of them can be adapted to younger or older children. After all, you know your grandchildren and will be able to pick and choose the activities you will enjoy together.

As you read through this book, you will find that some of the ideas and activities are variations of things you may have thought of or done already; they will serve as reminders as you plan. You will find lots of fun new things to do as well. As you read these ideas, you will probably be inspired to think of new things. There is no perfect recipe for developing a wonderful relationship with your grandchildren.

Of course, you will want to remember to abide by the parents' rules. It is important for the parents to feel comfortable that you won't wander far from what they value. Now, that doesn't mean you can't use your judgment about relaxing a nighttime bedtime or always serving the most nutritious meals. Just don't overdo things in an effort to be your grandchild's friend.

Each relationship is different… and wonderful… in its own way. Babysit. Share family stories. Sing songs, bake cookies, visit bookstores. Play games. Wipe some tears. LISTEN CAREFULLY.

MAKE MEMORIES and HAVE FUN.

Jana and Lynn

INDOORS

In The Kitchen

Kids can learn so much when you cook together. They learn about science, nutrition, measurements, and healthy eating. They can also benefit from the family lore that is often passed down in the kitchen. There are so many recipes that are easy enough for children to help and they can be given the easy chores for even more complicated dishes.

Enroll in a Cooking Subscription Service

Some programs provide all the ingredients along with the recipe and specific instructions. Some examples are: Hello Fresh, Home Chef, and Blue Apron. Though the preparation does take some time, the directions are clear. With guidance, children can learn about nutrition and different cooking methods. The services allow for choices in meal planning.

Kidstir is a program designed for kids aged 5-10. Each Happy Cooking Kit focuses on seasonal ingredients and special occasions.

Kids learn essential kitchen skills along the way. Each month, you receive three recipes and two appropriately sized cooking tools. A cookbook binder is included the first month. You receive the shopping list by email before the box arrives. This is a nice way for your grandchild to save some recipes and have their own cooking tools. Subscriptions can be purchased for 3 months, 6 months, 12 months at a time. Each kit also includes some fun games and puzzles. This would be most appropriate for grandparents who live near their grandchildren. Of course, it could also be a great birthday or holiday gift if the parent is willing to participate.

Make Rainbow Colored Ice Cubes
Ingredients

- 2 cups water
- Liquid food coloring, any color, either regular or neon colors

Directions

1. Add food coloring to water in a glass measuring pitcher (or other clear glass container) one drop at a time until you get the color you want. Mix food colors to make custom hues, if desired.

2. Pour colored water into compartments of an ice cube tray and freeze solid, about 2 hours or more.

Decorate a Fun Cake

If grandchildren live nearby, it might be possible to take a cake decorating class together. Otherwise, there are idea books and instructions online.

Lynn made this Big Bird cake, much to the delight of her young great granddaughter.

If you haven't used fondant, you might want to give it a try. It is like edible playdough. Big Bird's beak is made from fondant – colored with the same color as the feathers (feather effect made by using a "grass" tip)

Fondant is edible, but some people don't like it; however, it is fun to work with. You can roll it out and use cookie cutters or small shape molds to cut out shapes to use on other bake projects like the flowers and leaves on this "hat."

Make Buckeyes or Buckeye Fudge

These yummy treats are popular… and so easy.

Ingredients:

- 12 oz. peanut butter (creamy)
- ½ c. butter, softened
- 1 tsp. vanilla
- 4 c. powdered sugar
- 16 oz. semi-sweet chocolate…. or chocolate chips
- ¼ c shaved paraffin wax (optional)

Directions:

Using a mixer with a paddle attachment, beat the peanut butter and butter. Stir in vanilla. Add powdered sugar. Beat until smooth. Roll into small (1 inch or so) balls. Put on a cookie sheet and place in freezer until firm. Place the chocolate and wax in a deep bowl and microwave for 15 seconds at a time….stirring each time until mixture is melted. Dip the ball into the melted chocolate, leaving the top peanut butter showing (so the balls will look like buckeye nuts). Store in the refrigerator.

HINT: A cocktail fork or a couple of firm toothpicks will work for the dipping.

FUDGE:

When you don't want to mess around with rolling and dipping, just make fudge.

Ingredients:

    Peanut Butter Layer:

- 1 c. butter
- 1 c. peanut butter (creamy preferred)
- 1 tsp. vanilla
- 3 ½ cups powdered sugar

    Chocolate Layer:

- 7 oz. sweetened condensed milk (½ of a 14 oz. can)
- 1 ½ cups dark or semi-sweet chocolate chips
- 2 TBSP butter

How to… in the Microwave

Combine the peanut butter, butter and vanilla in a glass bowl and melt in microwave for 90 seconds. Stir. Mixture will be smooth and creamy. Slowly add the powdered sugar a cup at a time. Stir to combine.

Grease a 9-inch pan.

Spoon the peanut butter mixture into the pan … press evenly.

For the chocolate layer: Combine milk, chocolate, and butter in a medium sized glass bowl. Heat in microwave for 90 seconds. Stir and then heat another 15 seconds if necessary. Pour over the peanut butter fudge. Let the whole thing cool on the counter for several hours. Fudge can be chilled in the refrigerator to speed up the process. (Recipes from a friend of Jana's who lived in Ohio many years ago.)

Halloween Hot Dog Mummies

Ingredients
- 1 can (8 oz) Pillsbury™ refrigerated crescent rolls or 1 can (8 oz) Pillsbury™ refrigerated Crescent Dough Sheet
- 2 ½ slices American cheese, quartered (2.5 oz)
- Cooking spray

Photo courtesy of Sarah Donahue

- 10 hot dogs (NOTE: Try mini version with cocktail sausages.
- Mustard or ketchup, if desired

Directions

1. Heat oven to 375°F.
2. If using crescent rolls: Unroll dough; separate at perforations, creating 4 rectangles. Press perforations to seal. If using dough sheet: Unroll dough; cut into 4 rectangles.
3. With knife or kitchen scissors, cut each rectangle lengthwise into 10 pieces, (40 pieces of dough). Slice cheese slices into quarters.
4. Wrap 4 pieces of dough around each hot dog and 1/4 slice of cheese to look like "bandages," stretching dough slightly to completely cover hot dog. About 1/2 inch from one end of each hot dog, separate "bandages" so hot dog shows through for "face." On ungreased large cookie sheet, place wrapped hot dogs (cheese side down); spray dough lightly with cooking spray.
5. Bake 13 to 17 minutes or until dough is light golden brown and hot dogs are hot. With mustard, draw features on "face."

Recipe By Pillsbury Kitchens (www.pillsbury.com)

Meatloaf Foot

Using your favorite meatloaf recipe, shape the loaf into a foot shape. Use pieces of onion for the "nails."

Garnish with onion rings.

Photo from Pinterest

Vomiting Pumpkin

Cut open the top of a medium sized pumpkin. Remove the seeds. Cut slits for eyes and round hole for the mouth. Can add slight cut-out for nostrils.

Place the pumpkin on a serving tray and spoon the guacamole into pumpkin and pouring out of mouth. Serve with tortilla chips.

Photo courtesy of Adriane Pope

Easy Guacamole dip

Combine avocado, salsa, and lime juice. If you prefer something a bit spicier, you can add tomatoes, limes, onions, garlic powder and some red-hot seasoning.

Candy Corn Jello

Directions

1. Make lemon gelatin according to directions.
2. Add 1/3 cup to glasses and refrigerate for 2 hours or until firm.
3. Make the orange gelatin while the lemon gelatin is in the refrigerator.
4. Slowly pour 1/3 cup orange gelatin on top of the yellow. ...
5. Add a layer of whipped cream and top with a candy corn… (or 2!)

Photo and recipe from https://www.foodlion.com/recipes/candy-corn-jello

Easter Bunny Cake

When Jana was a teenager, she and her brother found a recipe for an Easter Bunny Cake in an old Betty Crocker cookbook. She also made one of the cakes for her own children when they were little. Her friend, Mona Bowden, makes one every year. Her grandchildren look forward to seeing their bunny cake's personality.

Use your favorite cake and icing recipes... or use boxed mixes. Carrot cake mix would be a great choice. Make two round 9" cakes.

To assemble: Leave one cake whole and place it on a large platter. Cut 2 opposite edges of the other layer into "ears." You will have the bow tie remaining. Arrange on the platter. Spread with frosting and decorate with shredded coconut, licorice, and candies. Your bunny will have its own personality!

Cut one of the 9" round cakes to form the bunny parts:

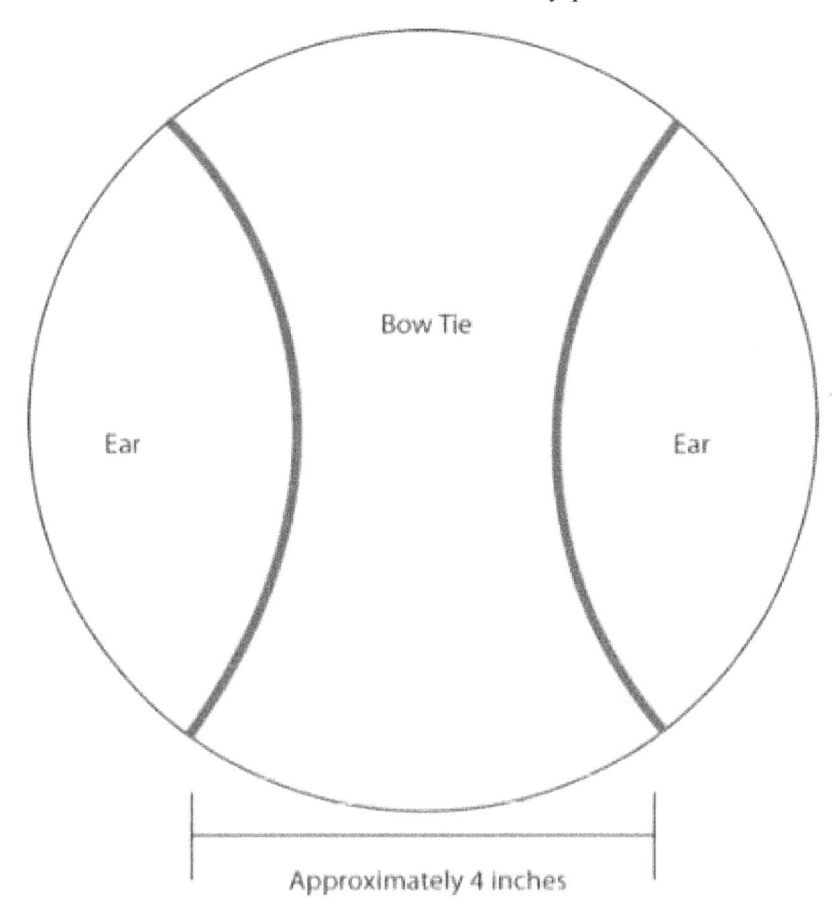

Bow Tie

Ear   Ear

Approximately 4 inches

Pattern from the 1970's---- Ganz Parent Club

April Fools Dessert Sliders

Let the kids make a spoof dessert that looks like a sandwich. Use cupcakes for the bun. Place a drop of sugar water to hold a few sesame seeds. The burger is a chocolate cookie. The mustard is a tinted piping of icing. The pickle is a kiwi sliced with a crinkle cutter. The ketchup is, of course, a dollop of icing tinted red.

Photo and recipe courtesy of Lorie Busby

Cinnamon Applesauce Ornaments

Picture courtesy of McCormick.com

Ingredients

- 1 c. applesauce
- 1 (4 oz.) container ground cinnamon
- 2 T. white liquid glue (such as Elmer's glue)

Directions

1. Mix the applesauce, cinnamon and glue until it is well combined.
2. Roll out the dough or just press down with your hands. The dough should be about ½' thick.

3. Press a cookie cutter into the dough to cut out your ornament. Gingerbread men shaped cutters or hearts are wonderful, but you can use any shape.

4. Use a straw or pencil to poke a hole near the top for a ribbon to hang the ornament.

5. Set the ornaments aside on waxed paper to dry…. This will take 3-4 days, or you can dry them in a 200-degree oven for a few hours.

NOTE: The cinnamon ornaments will dry exactly how they look when they are cut. If you want a smooth look, be sure to knead the dough until it is smooth.

IMPORTANT: These are NOT edible.

Valentine's Day Cookie Pizza

Ingredients

- 16 ½ ounce roll refrigerated sugar cookie dough, cut into 1/4-inch-thick slices
- 1 cup semisweet chocolate pieces (6 ounces)
- ½ cup creamy peanut butter, melted
- 1 ½ cups red and white candy-coated milk chocolate pieces
- Sprinkles

Directions

Press cookie dough slices into a greased 13-inch pizza pan. Bake in a 350 degrees F oven 15 to 20 minutes or until golden. Immediately sprinkle with chocolate pieces; let stand to soften, then spread chocolate evenly over crust. Drizzle melted peanut butter over chocolate. Sprinkle with red and white candy-coated milk chocolate pieces and sprinkles. Makes 12 servings

(From bhg.com/recipe/bar/holiday-cookie-pizza)

Turkey Cupcakes

Decorate cupcakes to look like turkeys. Cover the cupcake in base color icing (dark brown in the photo). Add a circular mound of icing near an edge to serve as the head, then use bits of candy to make the feathers in back and features on the head. Ideally you would have left over candy corn to stand up (point down) in the back. For this batch, Lynn didn't have candy corn, so she stood up various colors of M&Ms. She cut yellow M&Ms in half to use for the eyes and a small piece of red Swedish Fish to use as the waddle.

24

In The Craft Room

Create Your Own Picture Book

Using pictures you take of your grandchild and a favorite stuffed animal, write a book about them doing all the favorite things you and your grandchild do. For example, if you and your grandchild like to bake cookies, stage a picture of the stuffed animal baking cookies. When Lee Peace's niece left her favorite stuffed dinosaur at Lee's house, she took a series of pictures including the dinosaur reading books with Katie the dog, the dinosaur playing a game, the dinosaur watching a favorite show on TV, and the dinosaur on the niece's favorite riding toy. She then put the pictures together and used one of the photo services (Shutterfly, Apple, Walgreens, Walmart, etc.) to publish a book.

Photo courtesy of Lee Peace

Make a Scrapbook of a Parent Growing Up

Go through family albums and find cute pictures of your son or daughter (your grandchild's parent) growing up. Make copies and put them together in a scrapbook for your grandchild to give as a present. You will enjoy the time spent putting the book together, and your son or daughter will enjoy their special book for years to come.

Sample scrapbook page

Make a Keepsake Book of Cards

If you have ever wondered what to do with all the cards children receive for their birthdays, Valentine's Day, etc., here is a VERY simple idea.

1. Collect all the cards.
2. If desired, make a cover sheet: Johnny's First Birthday, Mary's First Valentine's Day, etc.
3. Using a hole punch, poke holes in an evenly spaced pattern... 2-3 holes will work well.
4. Tie ribbons through the holes. You could also use twisty-ties or metal key chains.

Photo from Pinterest

Create Art with Raised Salt Painting

This art activity appeals to everyone from toddlers to teens.

You need a few things to get started:

- card stock (or cardboard, paper plates, poster board),
- glue,
- salt,
- paint brush or cotton swab, such as a Q-tip
- watercolors.
- If you don't have liquid watercolors on hand, just make your own by watering down food coloring.

Directions:

1. First--Squeeze a glue design or a picture on the card stock.
2. Second—Sprinkle well with salt. Cover the glue.
3. Third—Tip the paper so the extra salt will fall away.
4. Fourth—Dip your paintbrush into the paint and GENTLY touch the salt lines. The paint will spread out in both directions so be sure to touch softly.
5. Finally—Let the art dry.

HINT: Place art in a baking dish or cookie sheet with raised sides when working on it so you can catch the extra salt when it falls away.

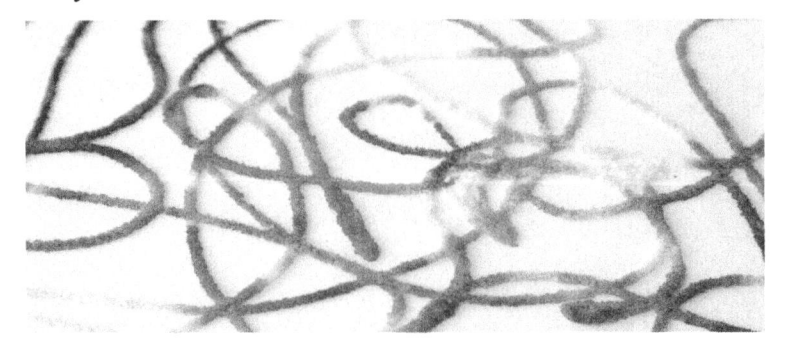

Create Art String Painting or Pulled String Art

This is another favorite art project for a wide range of ages to enjoy. The idea came from *a handbook of arts and crafts* by Philip Wigg and Jean Hasselschwert, published in 1968.

You will need:

- Paint in a small bowl (BioColor paint or tempera paint)
- String or yarn
- Paper

Directions:

HINT: Keep a bowl of warm soapy water and a cloth rag near so you can wash hands between steps.

1. Cut a piece of string and swirl it around in the bowl of paint. Use a disposable spoon or your fingers.
2. Lift the string, running your thumb and forefinger along the length of the string to remove excess paint.
3. Arrange the string on a piece of paper... be sure to let the end of the string hang out of the bottom edge.
4. Cover with a second piece of paper.
5. Place something heavy over the paper. A book or a box or heavy pan would work.
6. Pull the string out slowly.
7. Remove the weight and the top piece of paper and admire the artwork.
8. Let dry.

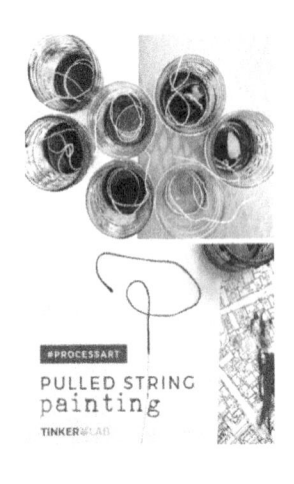

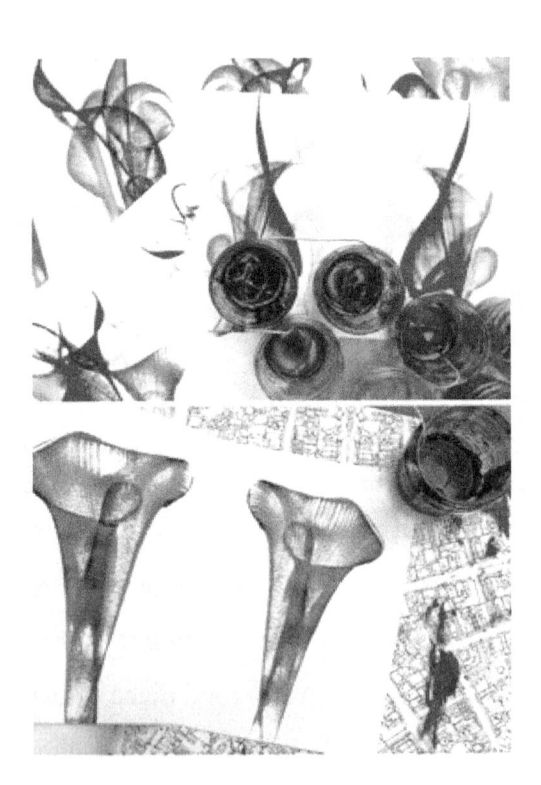

HINT: go to *www.artfulparent.com* to see the step by step directions in a video.

Make Perler Bead Bowls

In *Cousins Camp 2.0* there are directions for playing with Perler Beads and making designs. Jana is sure these Perler Bead Bowls will be popular at next year's Cousins Camp!

Directions

1. Using an ovenproof bowl, spray the interior of the bowl with PAM (or similar product) spray.
2. Drop Perler Beads into the bowl. Keep adding beads until they start to climb up the bowl... but keep them in one layer.
3. Once the bowl is filled to your satisfaction, bake it at 375 for approximately 12-15 minutes.
4. The plastic will begin to melt and the beads will stick together.
5. Watch the time carefully... ovens vary, and you don't want to burn the bowl.
6. Let the bowl cool on a rack.
7. Slide the Perler Bead Bowl out of the ovenproof bowl.

HINT: There will be a smell as the plastic melts. You may want an open window and an active fan so the whole house doesn't smell!

Image from Crafty Girl on YouTube

https://www.youtube.com/watch?v=bTRKEpQMfS0

Make Paper Snowflakes

1: First, begin with a square piece of copy **paper**.

2: Fold the square of **paper** diagonally to make a triangle.

3: Fold in Half Again.

4: Fold One Third.

5: Fold Again.

6: Cut the "top" Off at an Angle.

7: Shape It!

8: Unfold to see the snowflake.

For those of you who prefer a pattern for your snowflakes, *Snowflakes for all Seasons* has 72 cut and fold snowflakes by Cindy Higham.

Make Multi-Colored Coffee Filter Bowls

Supplies

- spray Starch (Faultless Premium Starch is perfect)
- water colors
- coffee filters
- paint brush

How To

Spread a coffee filter flat (put on paper towel or old newspaper).

Paint the coffee filter with as many different colors as you like.

(If you would like a less perfect round bowl, just cut a few edges so it won't look as much like a coffee filter!)

Place a cup or small bowl upside down.

Drape the filter over the cup and spray well with the starch. Though it is hard to see in the above picture, the colors will run a bit and look terrific.

Let the bowl dry thoroughly.

Create Tissue Paper Stained Glass

Stained glass is beautiful. If you have the skills and the proper equipment, you may want to complete a stained-glass project with your grandchild. If you are looking for something a little easier, there are many kits on the market. Check out any crafts store, Oriental Trading Company, and Amazon for a wide variety.

If you want something even easier, try a tissue paper project. To make a heart, follow these directions:

You will need

- tissue paper (for hearts use pink, red and white)
- construction paper (for hearts, use pink, red and white)
- clear contact paper
- scissors
- tape OR hole punch and string (optional)

Instructions:

1. Cut pink, red and white tissue paper in approximately 1/2 to 1-inch squares.
2. Fold a sheet of construction paper in half and cut out a large heart. You can unfold the heart to check out the shape. Refold it to make any adjustments.
3. While the heart is still folded, make a parallel cut about 1" inside the heart. This will give you your window frame. Save the inside heart cutout to make a smaller version later.
4. Open the heart and center it on a piece of contact paper.

5. Place the squares of tissue paper inside the heart on the contact paper.
6. Be careful not to go over the edge of the window frame. When the heart is filled with tissue paper, place a second piece of contact paper over the whole thing. Be careful not to make any air bubbles.
7. Cut away the excess contact paper. If you leave a little bit around the edge of the heart, it will stick together better.
8. You can now either tape your heart in a window or use a hole punch at the top and hang it with string.

Eloise and Lucille LOVED doing their stained-glass project. The only hard part was peeling the contact paper!

These directions are from Kimara Wise of Wee Folk Art and found on the web at Ticketmob.com

Experiment with More Stained Glass Projects

Smartschoolhouse.com provides directions for framed glass art.

You will need

- Picture frame with glass and removable backing
- Elmer's glue
- Gel food coloring
- Q-tips
- Paper plate or paper towels
- Extra fine glitter (optional)

DIY kids stained glass art

Directions:

1. Carefully remove the backing from the frame(s).
2. Place the glass on a paper plate or paper towel.
3. Squeeze glue onto one side of the glass.
4. Show your grandchild some colorful pictures for inspiration.
5. Pick out 4-6 colors using the gel food coloring.
6. Put a little bit of food coloring on the end of a q-tip.
7. Mix the glue and the food coloring with the q-tips until the glass is completely painted (as seen in the video).
8. Sprinkle on some extra fine glitter (optional).
9. Let the glass dry overnight.
10. Put the glass into the frame (without the backing) and display it in front of light.

Make Sea Glass Vases

This is another super easy craft. Just mix Elmer's Glue with a couple drops of food coloring. Paint it on anything glass; it will create a sea glass effect. Blue and green are perfect, but red and yellow will look great also.

Vases: http://justanotherhangup.blogspot.com/2015/07/diy-sea-glass-vases.html

Make Paper Corner Bookmarks

You will need:
- Assorted origami papers
- Scrapbook paper scraps
- Glue stick
- Yarn scraps
- Google eyes
- Hole punch
- Black marker

https://www.redtedart.com

Directions:

1. Fold square piece of paper in half. Bring corners up to top to make a triangle.
2. Open up and lay triangle flat. Bring top corner to center. Fold in sides and tuck under to form a square.
3. Cut smaller square for inside of bookmark. Glue in place.
4. Punch holes and add yarn. (not shown in above photo).
5. Add scrap paper shapes for arms, ears and horn for a unicorn.
6. Draw on mouth and nose.
7. Glue google eyes in place.

Directions based on Jo-Ann Stores,LLC; to see more pictures of bookmarks go to https://www.joann.com and search for "bookmarks."

Make Fingerprint Art Glass Magnets

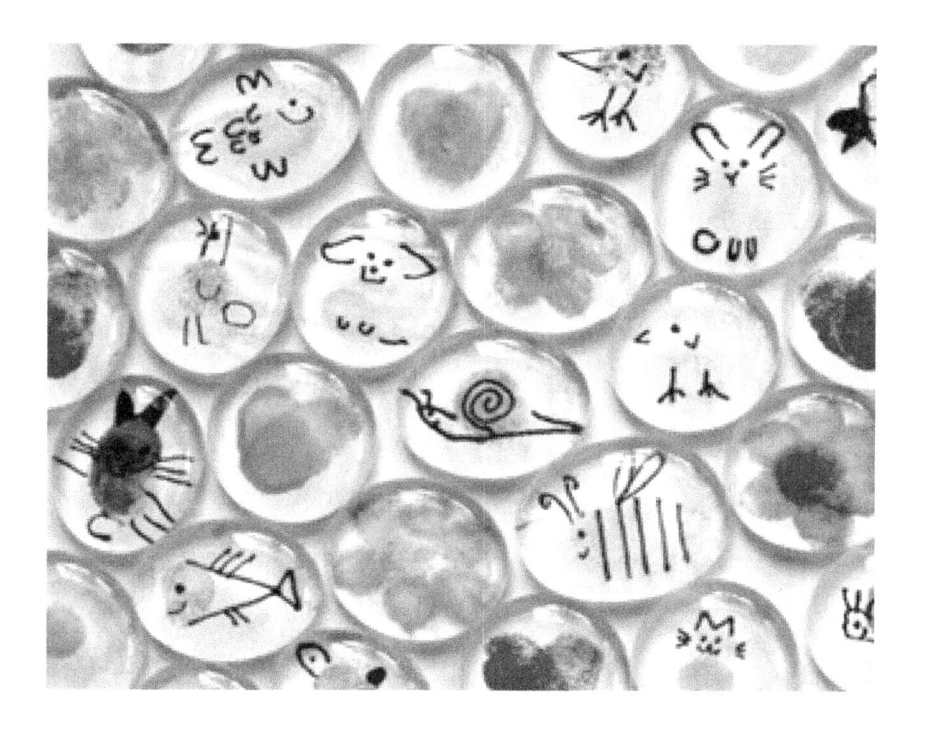

Materials:

- Paper (Use heavyweight printer paper.)
- Black fine tip permanent marker
- Finger ink pads
- Clear glass gems, extra-large flat back marbles, and clear glass cabochons. Make sure there is no coating on them. These can be purchased at most craft stores, some florists, and, of course, Amazon.
- Scissors
- Clear drying glue
- Magnets

What to Do:

Use thumbs to make hearts for thumbprint heart glass magnets:

1. Press a thumb into a finger ink pad.
2. Gently press the thumb (with the ink) onto paper.
3. Press thumb into ink pad again.
4. Tilt thumb slightly and press down… make a heart.
5. Allow the ink to dry.
6. Place a drop of the glue on the flat side of the glass gem.
7. Put a glass gem on top of the heart--glue side down.
8. Allow the glue to dry overnight.
9. Using small scissors, cut the paper away from the outer edge of the gem.
10. Use a foam brush to paint clear drying glue on top of the heart art paper on the back of the glass gem. Go over the edges of the paper to make sure they are glued down.
11. Place the magnet into the glue and allow to dry.

Using the picture above...or your own creativity...come up with other designs for your magnets.

Make Decorative Clipboards

Another great idea from Jo-Ann Stores is the decorative clipboard. Teens and tweens will love these. They are also great gifts.

JOANN.COM® is a registered trademarks of Jo-Ann Stores, LLC

Supplies & Tools:

- Clip board
- Assorted papers
- Assorted Washi tape
- Assorted ribbons
- Paper punch- optional
- Gold spray paint- optional
- Jar of Mod Podge- matte finish
- Painter's tape
- Sheet of printer paper
- Adhesive letter or stencils
- Bottle of Tombow glue (with the blue lid)
- Metal ruler
- Cutting surface

Directions:

1. Use painter's tape (or masking tape) to cover the area around the clip so you can spray paint it gold without getting paint on the clipboard. Let it dry. Otherwise, just leave it silver.
2. With the piece of white printer paper, make a cutting stencil to fit your paper around the clipboard so that when you cut out your decorative paper it will fit exactly around the metal clip when you glue it down.
3. Using the stencil trace the outline on the backside of your decorative paper. Cut it out with your metal ruler and x-acto knife.
4. Brush Mod Podge on the top part of the clipboard around the metal clip. Slide the paper in under and around the clip while it is still wet. Press the paper firmly around the clip.
5. Lift up the rest of the paper and apply the Mod Podge down the rest of the clipboard.
6. Press the paper firmly in place.
7. Apply decorative tape, trim, Washi tape to enhance your clip board.
8. Apply your letter or using the stencils paint a letter onto the finished clip board surface.
9. Attach ribbons at the top of the metal clip.

Have Fun with Fleece

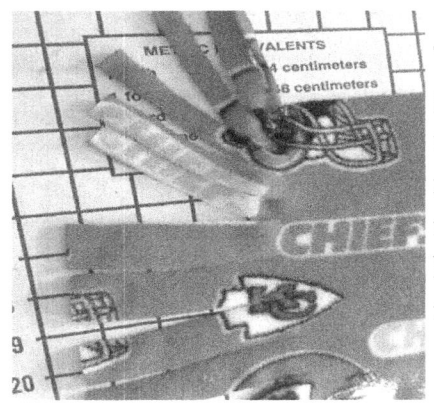

Make a No Sew Fleece Scarf

This is especially fun for a grandchild who is in to a sports team or hobby. Fleece comes in many print designs including many of the team logos for the NFL. The photo shows a scarf made for a KC Chiefs fan.

Buy at least 1/4 yard (9 inches or 22.86 cm) of the fabric of your choice. Fleece comes in a variety of thicknesses and patterns. Lynn likes to buy a little extra - to be sure she can line up any recurring pattern in the fleece.

1. Lay the fabric on a large table.
2. Fold the fabric in half along the length of the fabric matching up the curled edges on the ends as closely as possible.
3. Smooth out the fabric with your hands. If there is a recurring pattern in the fleece, square up the edge to show a straight line of the pattern.
4. Measure the width and length of your favorite type of scarf. Scarf length preference varies from person to person, so the size is your decision. 8 or 9 inches (21 to 23 cm) is a standard width for a scarf. 60 inches (152.4 cm) is a standard length for a scarf. 40 inches (102 cm) long would work

better for a child. (The width of fleece is typically 60" wide.)

5. Measure the preferred width from the straightened edge of your fleece several times along the length, then cut along the marks to end up with a long slender piece of fleece. Again, beware of a repeating pattern and cut so as to make the pattern line up with the side. Or use a straight edge or yardstick to connect the marks on the length of fabric that does not have a pattern.

6. Trim your fabric in line with your measurements, using a sharp pair of fabric scissors. HINT: decide if you should let child cut or do it for them for safety.

7. Cut off the white or curled (selvage) edges at the bottom of the scarf, while the length is still folded in half. Use a straight edge to ensure you cut evenly.

8. Make a fringe on the ends of the scarf. Measure 5 inches (12.7 cm) from the edge of the bottom of the length of the scarf. Mark it with a pencil and draw a line to have consistent stopping point/length of fringe. You want the fringe of your scarf to be 5 inches (12.7 cm) long. Measure and cut the 5 inch (12.7 cm) strips every 1/2 inch (1.3 cm) or smaller, but be sure to be consistent in the width of the stripes. Lynn prefers to first cut 1" strips and then go back and cut them in half so as to obtain ½ inch fringe. This will complete the fringe and your no-sew fleece scarf is ready to use.

Make A No-Sew Pet Pillow Cover

If your grandchild has a pet (dog or cat) s/he will likely enjoy making something to be used and loved by their pet. This project can be used to recover an existing pillow or as a casing to be stuffed anew.

Complete instructions available at
http://www.craftibilities.com/2017/08/diy-large-dog-bed.html

Lynn prefers to use fleece, but any stretch fabric would work. You will need two identically sized pieces of fabric. She recommends using one print fabric and one solid contrasting color fabric.

Measure the length and width of the pillow you are covering and add 4 inches to each measurement so as to cut the fabric to cover the pillow while allowing for 4" ties to close the cover around the pillow. For example, if existing pillow is 36X30, you would cut fabric 40X34.

NOTE: if the pillow is round or oval there is no need to adjust for corners. If the shape is square or rectangular, you will want to cut a 4" square out of each corner before beginning to cut the fringe/ties to avoid unnecessary bulk at the corners.

1. Once the pieces are cut, lay them together with GOOD SIDES OUT. Measure from the outside of the fabric 4" in and mark. Do that all the way around the perimeter, then draw a line connecting all the marks to prepare for cutting the fringe to be used as ties.
2. Next cut (through both layers) from the outside to the line just drawn in ½" intervals to create the fringe/ties.
3. Remember: If your pattern is square or rectangular, you would have cut a 4" square out of each corner before preparing the fringe/ties.
4. Starting anywhere, begin to tie the patterned and solid fringe together (square knot recommended) all the way around leaving one end open to either insert the pillow or the new stuffing and finish tying off to close. If you are recovering a large pillow it is best to place the pillow between the 2 fabrics before you beginning tying. Go all around and make all the ties securing the contents and voila, you and you grandchild have just created a lovely pillow.

If you're making a new pillow, you might consider stuffing with old clothes rather than polyester stuffing.

NOTE: you can make any kind of pillow with this method, but pet pillows are a favorite. A "favorite team" fleece pillow is also a winner.

Make Fabric Wall "Art"

This is a quick and easy way to help your grandchild decorate/personalize their room. Create "art" with a fabric print chosen by your grandchild. The fabric can be stretched over a quilting hoop for a round picture or, for larger "prints," stretched over stretch bars and stapled on the back. Stretch bars are purchased in pairs and can be put together to accommodate almost any size. They can be found at craft stores or on line.

The fabric could be a large panel of their favorite character – especially nice for a toddler's room or a bizarre multicolor repeating pattern selected by a teen. In any case, you should get the parent's permission for this project.

You can find fabric by shopping at your local fabric store or search on line for "character fabric panel" or go to

https://4my3boyz.com/character-large-cotton-fabric-panels

Make Sun Melted Crayons

Materials:

- old crayons
- aluminum foil
- cookie cutters
- a paper plate

Directions:

1. Peel the paper from the crayons and break them into small pieces. Depending on the temperature of the day... the hotter the day, the bigger the crayon pieces can be.
2. Cover the plate with aluminum foil.
3. Place cookie cutters on the aluminum foil.
4. Add crayon bits inside the cookie cutters.
5. Wait for the sun to melt the crayons. This won't take long on a hot summer day. Temperatures above 100 degrees are perfect.
6. Take your "new" crayons inside where they can cool off. Then just push them out of the cookie cutters.
7. Color your next masterpiece.

Based on an activity from https://www.notimeforflashcards.com

Use Sun-Melted Crayons Art Activity

Materials:

- crayons
- cookie sheet
- waxed paper
- stones

or something to hold the paper down

Directions:

1. Take a piece of wax paper and fit it on a cookie sheet.
2. Place the sheet in the sun so it will heat.
3. When the foil feels warm, draw on it using your choice of crayons.
4. The foil heat will help melt the wax slightly, and the crayon will be easy to move around.
5. Try a stained-glass effect by outlining a shape and then use one color in each shape.
6. When you are finished, just peel the wax paper off the baking sheet.

Based on directions from happy hooligans art craft play https://happyhooligans.ca

Make a Leaf Rubbing

This can be as basic as you like or can include learning about the structure of a leaf and understanding the function of the various parts of the leaf.

There are a few great books you may want to read before you begin your leaf rubbing project:

- *Why Do Leaves Change Color?* This is part of the *Let's Read and Find Out Science* series
- *Autumn Leaves* by Ken Robbins
- *Fandex Family Field Guide to Trees* by Steven Aronson
- *Awesome Autumn* by Bruce Goldstone

You will need:

- leaves
- tracing paper
- parchment paper
- wax paper
- tin foil
- crayons
- colored pencils
- oil pastels
- a clipboard

How to:

- Place the leaf on a clip board.
- Cover the leaf with the paper you are using.
- Slowly, use the crayons, colored pencils, oil pastels and rub over the top of the paper to see the outline and details of the leaf.
- You can use the oil pastels with all three types of paper to see how it looks different based on the paper type. You can use all the drawing tools on one piece of paper to create a layered look.

This picture and activity are from the web site kcedventures.com

In The Game Room

(or living room or work room or kitchen – wherever you have a flat workspace.)

Make a Fort

This may be the oldest idea, but sometimes the old ideas are the best ones. Using blankets, pillows, sheets, kitchen chairs, a couch, drape the sheets and blanket over the area you want to cover. This is a great area to play house or curl up with a good book... or two.

Aria and Abi   *Photo courtesy of Mona Bowden*

Send a Postcard

Grandparents may think of sending postcards to their grandchildren when they are on vacation, but it is also a good way to stay in touch in the in-between times. Local stores may have postcard selections near the check-out lanes, and Amazon has a fun selection of sets. Jana sends history cards to the older grandchildren and fun animal cards to the younger ones. They ALL seem to love the Where's Waldo cards.

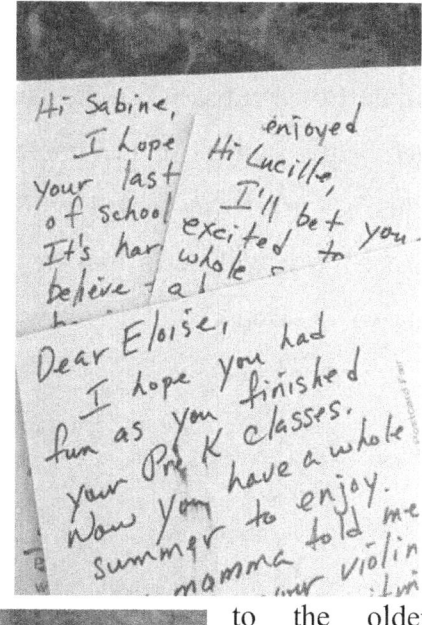

NOTE: Many schools no longer teach cursive writing; it may be a good idea to print your message.

Start a Tradition

Take a recurring picture

Mona Bowden has taken the same picture every other year when her family gathers at her home for Thanksgiving or Christmas. This is a great way to follow the grandchildren as they grow up. What fun it will be to look at the pictures when everyone is all grown up. Don't you love the way they posed the same way?

Apolo, Celia, Winnie, Aria

Photos courtesy Mona Bowden

Buy A Special Ornament Every Year

Every family enjoys special traditions. Children like to know what to expect at different times of the year. *In 100 Plus Things To Do With Your Grandchildren,* there are sections on completing a yearly questionnaire (page 73) and having a yearly 1:1 birthday lunch page 87). Though Jana just began buying Christmas ornaments for each child, they liked the ornaments so much, she plans to do that every year. For 2018, the oldest grandchildren received driver's license ornaments because they are each getting ready to drive on their own. (Now that is a scary thought!)

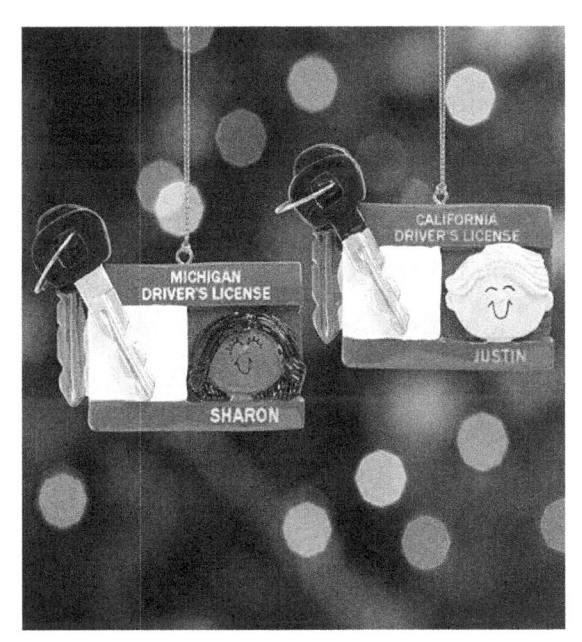

These ornaments came from Personal Creations (*www.personalcreations.com/*) and were a big hit. Of course, they had the correct state and child's name! You will be able to find ornaments for every sport and interest your grandchildren may have.

Play Picture This

Each person gets a paper plate and a marker. They have to hold the plate on their head with one hand and draw their name and something they like with the other. Set a timer. If anyone can guess what the drawing is, they win. Give a small prize.

Draw Partner Pictures

Partners sit back to back... so they cannot see what their partner is drawing or has on their paper. One person draws a simple line drawing and then tries to get their partner to duplicate it using verbal directions only. Compare drawings to see if they are at all similar. (NOTE: They probably won't be which will make everyone laugh.) Change partners and/or who gives the directions.

It may be a good idea to have several line drawings ready to use so the game doesn't get bogged down immediately. In that case, one partner gives verbal directions, and the other partner does the drawing.

Play Individualized Bingo

Go to *myfreebingocards.com* to generate your own set of Bingo cards, including a card to cut up for the announcer.

Jana generated a set for a talk to grandparents at a local library.

- Enter your own bingo words, and the bingo card generator will randomize them and create custom bingo cards for you.
- There is a choice of themes.
- The bingo cards are created in PDF format, so they are easy to print and you can save them and share them.

Play Candy Ball - Saran Wrap Version

In *Cousins Camp 2.0*, there are directions for a candy ball using bubble wrap. This has been one of the favorite activities for the Hletko cousins every summer. In that version, the ball is composed of multiple layers of bubble wrap, and the idea is to rip the wrap apart in order to get to the candy/treats in the ball. In the Saran Wrap version, the idea is to CAREFULLY remove each layer of Saran Wrap WITHOUT RIPPING IT. If Wrap is ripped, ball goes immediately to next player.

The Saran Wrap Ball Game Rules:

The first person with the ball starts unwrapping the ball while the person on their right rolls a pair of dice, trying to roll doubles. If you prefer, you could pick a specific number ... 7 or 11 perhaps.

Once doubles are rolled, the ball is passed to the next player and the sequence begins again.

The person with the ball does not stop unwrapping until the person to their right rolls doubles. This creates an urgency to the game! You want to roll the dice over and over again as quickly as you can so you get the ball!

You get to keep the treasures you unwrap!

Tips:

Start with the oldest child first so that the younger ones can see what to do before it's their turn.

A bell of some sort is fun in the middle because that adds to the noise... and the excitement.

Besides candy, you can pack gift cards, money, small toys, a deck of cards. Use a metal cookie tin lid to add to the excitement… and to keep the dice contained.

Play Heads or Tails

This is a great activity if you are waiting in line somewhere or just need a filler for a few minutes.

Players put a hand on either their head or their "tail." Flip a coin. If it's heads, then the tails are out. If it's tails, then the heads are out. The last person wins the coin.

Play Twizzler Knot

This is another quick game perfect to take a few minutes while you are waiting for a meal or getting ready to go somewhere. Place everyone into groups of two and hand them ten Twizzlers (make sure they are fresh).

The goal for each team is to tie the Twizzler into a knot (a simple loop that is pulled together is fine). The catch is that they must work together as a team, but each participant can only use one hand.

The first team to tie up all ten Twizzlers wins a package of Twizzlers!

HINTS:

1. Use Twizzlers, not licorice. Twizzlers are more slippery and more durable as well.

2. Have some extra Twizzlers around in case that some break.

Work on a Crossword Puzzle Together

There are lots of books with puzzles of various degrees of difficulty. Your local newspaper may publish one each day. When you are ready, the *New York Times* has a great puzzle daily. Start with the Monday and Tuesday versions and work your way up to the weekend puzzles. Practice really does help because so many of the clues/answers repeat. You can also try teen magazines or *People* magazine.

For the younger set, check out:

http://activities.raisingourkids.com/crossword-puzzles/001-crossword-puzzle.html

Start with a blank and make up your own with clues you know your grandchild would like/know to get them into playing word games.

https://www.word-game-world.com/blank-crossword-puzzles.html

Create a Family Tree or Website

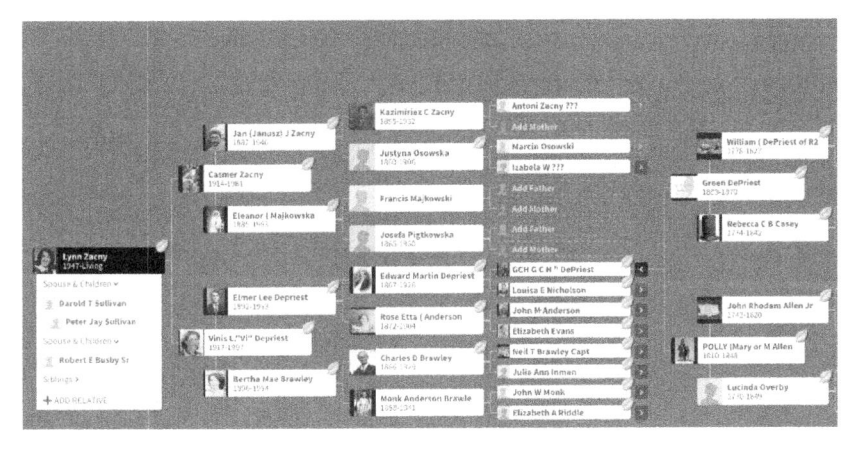

Screenshot of part of Lynn's family tree built using Ancestry.com

For over ten years, Lynn has been researching her family ancestry on her maternal side which dates back to 1689 and has discovered many interesting things in the process.

You might want to build a tree on commercially available applications like Ancestry.com. Building a tree and access to some databases is free but be aware of charges for access to its tremendous volume of resources for finding ancestors.

You might want to build a Website for your family to make your ancestry more public and in the hopes of finding family members outside of closed systems like Ancestry.com.

NOTE: There are ongoing costs involved with building and maintaining a website. If your grandchild is interested, you might volunteer to cover the costs and let them do the technical work with your help to organize the site and decide what content to have on it.

There are a couple of steps involved.

The first step is to get a "domain" name. Make the word unique to allow people to find your site. It typically costs about $10/year just to do a search and claim a unique domain name. There are several companies on line to help with claiming a domain name. Some offer an introductory price of $.99/year for the first year. You will likely have to try several combinations of your title name + extension to find one that is unique (a lot of the ".com" names have already been reserved.

The second step is to build the website. There are several companies that help you do that but beware this is where it can get expensive – example: though GoDaddy has lots of nice friendly features, it will nickel and dime you with every little feature.

WELCOME TO THE DEPRIEST FAMILY HERITAGE SITE

BEGINNING WITH ROBERT DEPRIEST, FRENCH HUGUENOT

Immigration to America   The DePriests were there   History in the making

You can make this a joint project with your grandchild by providing the content (old photos, stories, etc.) and let your tech savvy grandchild actually build the site with the content you provide. You will also need to think about how to organize a web site which typically has multiple "pages" and links built in.

Play Cards

Card games are a popular way for people of all ages to enjoy spending time together. A simple deck of cards can provide many ways of learning and playing together and the best part: no electricity required!

Panic

Directions:

You need one deck of cards for each player. HINT: It will help if the sets have different designs on the back so it will be easy to sort the cards at the end of the game.

Each player shuffles his cards. When one person says "begin" each player quickly deals five cards face up in a row in front of him. Then, he counts out 12 additional cards and places them face down next to the row of five cards. This is his reserve pile. He does not look at the reserve cards. The remainder of the deck are the extra cards and they stay face down in the player's hand.

The object of the game is to be the first player to get rid of all of the cards.

Everyone plays at once. If there is a card with the number two on it in the row of 5 cards in front of a player, the player places that card in the middle of the table. Any player can now add a card on top of the number two card by playing cards in numerical order. Continue placing cards on top of the stack in numerical order until the ace card is played. The person who laid that card on top of the pile places the stack to the side and out of the way. No more cards can be placed on top of it.

If a player takes a card from the row of five in front of him and places it on top of a stack of cards in the middle of the play, he takes a card from his reserve pile, turns it over, and places it face up in the row of five cards. A player must have five face-up cards in front of him at all times.

If a play cannot be made from the five cards that are facing up in front of the player, the player takes the extra cards in his hand, counts three cards, and turns them over placing them in a pile face up with only the top card exposed. The exposed card may now be played onto the center stacks of cards if it can be played in numerical order. If the card that is turned over is a number 2 card, it can be placed in the middle of the players to start a new pile of cards. If the exposed card in the hand is played, it will expose another card that may also be played. If that card is also played, another card is exposed and can be played.

If the exposed card cannot be played, an additional group of three cards is taken from the top of the extra cards held in the player's hand and turned over placing them on the pile allowing only the top card to show.

Players continue turning cards over from their hand (in groups of three) while looking for cards that can be placed on the piles in the center of play. When all the extra cards in the players hand have been turned over, the player quickly picks up the pile of extra cards, turns them over so they are face down in his hand, places the top card on the bottom of the deck, and begins again going through the deck, three cards at a time, playing only the top exposed card.

Speed is important! The more cards a player can turn over, the more cards the player can quickly place onto the center stacks. The faster the player goes, the sooner he will get rid of all of his cards. When a player has played all of his cards, the player yells "PANIC' and is the winner. This ends the game. Be sure to sort the cards so they will be ready to play later.

HINT: It might be a good idea to use old cards because cards will get bent as players become more aggressive.

Slap Jack

Use a standard 52-card pack. Young children can play, as long as they can recognize when a Jack is played.

The goal is to win all the cards, by being first to slap each jack as it is played to the center.

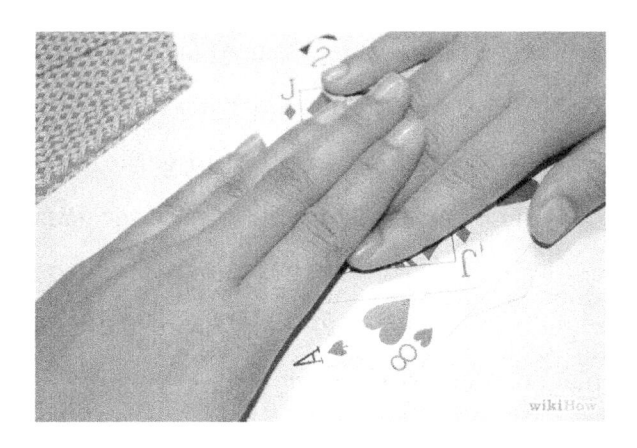

Deal cards one at a time face down, to each player until all the cards have been dealt. The hands do not have to come out even. Without looking at any of the cards, each player squares up his hand into a neat pile in front of them.

Beginning on the dealer's left, each player lifts one card at a time from their pile and places it face up in the center of the table.

When the card played to the center is a jack, the first player to slap their hand down on the jack takes it, as well as all the cards beneath it. The player winning these cards turns them face down, places them under their pile of cards, and shuffles them to form a new, larger pile.

When more than one player slaps at a jack, the one whose hand is directly on top of the jack wins the pile. If a player slaps at any card in the center that is not a jack, they must give one card, face down, to the player of that card. When a player has no more cards left, they remain in the game until the next jack is turned. The player may slap at the jack in an effort to get a new pile. If the player fails to win that next pile, they are out of the game.

HINT: It might be a good idea to use old cards because cards will get bent as players become more aggressive.

Spoons

This classic game has the fun of matching games with the excitement of musical chairs.

Materials Required:

- A standard deck of 52 playing cards, several spoons (one less than the total number of players).

Number of Players: 4-8 is recommended.

Length of Game: Games are fairly quick – about 5-10 minutes per game.

Have everyone sit in a circle, facing each other. Shuffle the deck of cards. Place spoons in the middle---have one less than the number of players; in other words, if there are five players, then four spoons should be in the middle of the circle.

Deal each player four cards. Put the remaining cards in a stack. The first player takes a card from the deck and places it into his hand. He or she decides whether to keep this card or not. He or she quickly discards one card from his hand and passes it, face down, to the next person in the circle (in clockwise order).

The goal to try to get 4 of a kind. Once a person gets 4 of the same rank of card, he or she is now eligible to grab a spoon from the middle. Once anyone takes a spoon from the middle, the rest of the players can now grab a spoon, even if they don't yet have four of a kind. In order not to lose, you must grab a spoon in time. The last player (the one who was not successful in getting a spoon) loses and is out of the game. Take one spoon away and repeat this process until there is only one winner left.

HINT: A good strategy is to pause for a moment when other players are distracted before quietly taking a spoon. You can also fake out other players by pretending to reach for a spoon without actually touching one. If a person erroneously grabs a spoon when no one has 4 of a kind, they also lose.

War

This simple game is good for very young grandchildren to learn the value of cards – e.g. Queen beats Jack. Good for 2-3 players.

How to Play

1. Deal all 52 cards out to the players.
2. Each person turns up one card and the highest card takes the trick (all of the cards played in that round).
3. If two people turn over the same value card, such as 3's, 8's, or Jacks, there is a WAR.
4. In a war, each player places three cards face down and then one more card face up. The highest card placed face up wins that round and takes all the cards played.
5. Players continue to turn their cards upside down and keep going until someone is out of cards. If three people are playing, the other two continue until second player is out of cards.
6. Continue rounds until all cards are played.

The winner is the one who collects all the cards.

https://www.wikihow.com/Play-War-(Card-Game)

Play Dice Games

Drop Dead

Though the name may be unfortunate, this fast-paced dice game is fun for any age group and can be played anywhere.

Game Objective: score as many points as possible. Decide if the goal is a target score, such as 50 or 100 or how many rounds should be played.

Materials Required:

- Sets of 5 six-sided dice. This is a great use for the dice from a Tenzi game so everyone gets a different color. For example, if there are three people playing, you would need three sets of dice. However, it will also work to play with just one set of 5 regular dice, passing them around the table in turn.
- Pen and paper for keeping score.
- 2 or more players

Optional: throwing cups, like from a Yahtzee game. Or you can make your own from cardboard tubes and/or paper cups.

How to play:

Roll one die to see who goes first. The player with the highest roll starts.

Player one throws all five dice. If the roll contains a 5 or a 2 the player scores no points, removes any dice showing a 5 or 2 and re-rolls the remaining dice. If the roll does not contain a 5 or a 2, the player adds up the total, records it on the score card and rolls all five dice again. The player continues in this way until all the dice are removed from play. Play continues with the next player.

Example: First throw: Player rolls a 3-5-2-6-4. No score, remove the 5 and 2. Second throw: Re-rolls remaining three dice. Rolls a 3-4-1. Score: 8 Third throw: Rolls the same three dice. Rolls a 2-

2-4. No score, removes the two dice showing a 2. Fourth throw: Rolls remaining 1 die. Rolls a 6. Score: 6. Fifth throw: rolls 1 die. Rolls a 5. No score. Total score: 8+6= 14

Pig

Pig is a fast dice game of chance. All you need to play is 2 players (or more) and 1 die.

To play Pig, a player rolls the die over and over. The goal is to get as many points as possible by adding up the face value of the rolls. But watch out: if you roll a 1, your turn is over, and you lose all of the points from that roll.

Keep rolling and chance losing your points - or play it safe and pass the die to the next player and keep all the points you rolled. In other words, don't be a pig.

The first player to reach 100 points wins.

Play the Candy Bar Game

You will need:
- A candy bar for each player
- one spoon and one butter knife for each player
- one pair oven mitts
- a silly hat, sunglasses, apron, a boa if you have one
- pair of dice

To Play:

Each player should have a candy bar and a spoon and dull knife in front of them.

Put all the other supplies/props in the middle of the table.
The youngest player should go first. The player gets to roll the dice 5 times in an effort to get doubles. If the player does roll doubles, he/she must grab the gear in the middle of the table and put it all on. The player will try to open and eat their candy bar.

The other players in turn get 5 tries to roll doubles. Immediately upon rolling doubles, that player takes all the gear from the other player...who must stop trying to open and eat their candy bar..., put it all on and begin working on opening and eating their candy bar. The dice keep getting passed around as players roll doubles and take the gear so they can try to open and eat their candy.

The first person to eat her entire candy bar while wearing the attractive gear you have provided is declared the winner. Then, everyone gets to enjoy their candy.

HINT: With younger children, you may want to let them get on their costume before the next player starts rolling the dice.

HINT: Use a small box to roll the dice. That beats chasing them all over the room! And the extra noise will add to the excitement.

HINT: Know your audience. If your grandchildren are not allowed to eat candy, this may not be a good game to play.

OUTDOORS (YARD/GARDEN/PARK)

Have a Scavenger Hunt

This is a fun game if you have enough people to divide into groups. Dividing into families is perfect.

Directions: Your family will have one hour to gather the items below and bring them back to the judges. The family with the most correct items will win a prize. The items do not have to be presented in the order they appear here. In other words, you may skip an item and move on. Your family can split up but must approach the judges as a team.

1. The more I dry, the wetter I become.
2. I don't go out and play, I just stay home all day, I'm nice – you might agree, but mostly your feet just rub me.
3. Stiff is my spine and my body is pale, but I'm always ready to tell a tale.
4. I have a ring, but no finger.
5. I have a neck, but no head, but I still wear a cap.
6. My words number quite many (like pen, pent, and penny); my title you will discover, is explained under my cover.
7. I start with an "e", I end with an "e", but I usually contain only one letter.
8. I'm so simple that I only point; yet I guide people all over the world.

9. Although I may have eyes, I can't see. At one time there was a dearth of me in Ireland and people went hungry.

10. I am black and white and "red" all over.

11. A rainbow in a box.

12. I am higher without a head, than with it.

13. I grow shorter as I grow older.

14. I have a face that doesn't frown, I have hands that do not wave, I have no mouth, just a familiar sound, I don't walk – but I move around? And... no... the judge did not allow the beer bottle to count for # 12!

Team I presents their results.

SCAVENGER HUNT answer sheet

1. Towel	2. Door-Mat
3. Book	4. Telephone
5. Bottle	7. Envelope
8. Compass	9. Potato
10. Newspaper	11. Box of Crayons/Markers
12. Pillow	13. Candle
14. Clock	

Have a Selfie Scavenger Hunt

You will need at least one adult in each group if you are going to be out and about.

Your team/family will have one hour to find and photograph the following items. The team with the most points will win a prize. Each item earns 1 point. Bonus points may be earned......

- All five of you are pictured... 1 point
- Have another family in your picture with you...... 2 points (cannot be related to you)
- Someone in your picture is wearing red... 1 point
- Someone in your picture is wearing a baseball cap... 2 points (can't be the same in more than one picture)
- Someone in your picture is wearing either a Nationals or a Cubs cap... 10 points (can't be the same cap in more than one picture) NOTE: Obviously, change the team to reflect your family choice.

For some extra fun, go to *upsidedowntext.com* to generate the directions for this hunt. You will just type in the content, and it will automatically appear upside down.

selfie with something bumpy (selfie with something bumpy)
selfie with something round (selfie with something round)
selfie with something red (selfie with something red)
selfie in front of a garbage can (selfie in front of a garbage can)
selfie with two kinds of leaves (selfie with two kinds of leaves)
selfie with street sign (selfie with street sign)
selfie with something smooth (selfie with something smooth)
selfie in front of yellow car (selfie in front of yellow car)
selfie in front of a tree (selfie in front of a tree)

Photo by Sarah Donahue

NOTE: Originally there was a requirement for a picture with a family they did not know but it has been left off this list. The teams found resistance when they asked for pictures including children.

NOTE: Be prepared for some good heated arguing. One team drew a picture of a yellow car and took the picture holding that. The judge decided not to allow.

Have a Balloon or Beach Ball Race

You need at least 4 people for this race. Stand two children side by side. Place a beach ball or a balloon between them. They have to race across the yard without dropping the ball/balloon. If it drops, they must go back to the starting line and begin again.

If you don't have four children, you may want to play this game as individuals. Then just place a balloon between each child's knees.

NOTE: This game could also be played with each child placing a potato between his knees. Place a bucket at the finish line so the potato can be deposited.

Play Feed a Cousin

This could be played in the kitchen, but since it can get quite messy, consider playing this game outside.

Pair the cousins. One cousin is blindfolded and tries to feed the partner cousin some sort of food using a spoon. Ice cream or baby food would be good choices.

SUGGESTION: It might be a good idea for the cousin being fed to wear goggles and a raincoat!

HINT: Make sure the cousin being fed sits still and doesn't move into the spoon! They can give verbal directions.

Go for a Detective's Walk
Look for :
- Clouds that look like shapes... a dog, a dragon, a kite, etc.
- Examine a cobweb.
- Fill a basket with nuts, leaves, sticks. When you get home, design a centerpiece for the table.
- Throw rocks in a river, stream, pond. See if you can make them skip.
- Draw pictures in the dirt.
- Take binoculars that you have made with two toilet paper rolls tied together with string.
- Find things that are your grandchild's favorite color.

Perform Random Acts of Kindness

Though grandparents do not usually have the main responsibility for teaching children how to be good people, it certainly teaches your values and reinforces what the parents are preaching at home if you serve as an example. Along these lines, there are many things you can do with your grandchildren to help them grow up to be sensitive, caring adults.

A few suggestions for acts of kindness:
- Hold the door open for someone.
- Let someone with just a few items behind you in line at the grocery line go ahead of you.

- Return a few carts in a grocery store parking lot.
- Take a small plant to a local nursing home and ask the receptionist to give it to someone who doesn't get many visitors.
- Leave a nice letter in a library book pointing out some of your favorite parts. (no names necessary)
- Help a neighbor rake leaves or shovel snow.
- Write a thank you note and leave a small treat (candy bar, bag of chips---something wrapped) to the mail carrier and leave in your mailbox.
- Pay for someone's lunch who is behind you in line at a fast food restaurant. This is even better if you are traveling at a holiday time and happen to see a soldier getting lunch. Thank them for their service and pay for their meal.
- Check in with an elderly neighbor and have a short visit.
- Obviously, the possibilities are endless. You and your grandchild will come up with specific ideas that will work best for you.

Go Horseback Riding (or Sponsor Lessons)

If you don't feel up to actually riding, try to visit a horseback riding stable. While your grandchild may be interested in some lessons, there is a lot to consider before you take that step. First of all, consider the safety aspects of horseback riding which would certainly require parental approval. Waivers have to be signed. Of course, proper equipment is a must... don't forget a helmet.

NOTE: You may want to consider that this is a very expensive hobby so you will want to check with the parents before even considering a trip to a stable. Jana has a friend who includes a few days of horse camp each summer when her granddaughter visits.

If you decide to go ahead, there are several online sites that could be a big help.

http://dullesmoms.com/horse/
https://www.horseshoenation.com/horseback-riding-lessons-choosing-instructor/
http://thehorseridingsite.com/how-to-choose-riding-school

Audrey with her favorite ride   *Photo courtesy Sarah Donahue*

Hold a Community Bike Wash

Have everything people need to wash their bikes. Another possibility is to wash the bikes for a small fee. Donating the money earned to a local charity would be a great idea.

You'll need:
- buckets
- dish soap
- brushes
- sponges
- rags

DO

• Recycle your dish sponges. You'll get another couple of months out of them on bike-wash duty.

• Floss with a clean rag between chainrings, cogs, and other hard-to-reach places.

• Be committed. A clean bike rides better and lasts longer.

DON'T

• Mix your buckets, tools, and rags. You don't want to cover your frame with drivetrain grease.

• Use an abrasive sponge or brush on your frame.

• Blast your bike with a high-pressure hose. Water will get into and degrade your bearings.

For step by step instructions on how to clean a bike, go to https://www.bicycling.com/repai/g20034545/how-to-clean-your-bike/

Do Some Gardening Together

This is a wonderful way to encourage your grandchild's curiosity and enthusiasm for the outdoors. It is easier to do this on an ongoing basis if your grandchild lives nearby, but if they live far away, you could plan for some time spent together doing a task while they are visiting. After they go back home, you could update the garden's status with pictures and notes.

Gardening can instill a sense of responsibility and pride which can lead to enthusiastic adult gardeners. Planting seeds, digging in the soil, pulling out weeds gets children involved. There are studies that show that when children have contact with soil during activities like digging and planting, they have improved moods and better learning experiences. Gardening may even lead to decreased anxiety.

Gardening can aid fine motor development which will lead to academic skills like writing, cutting, typing and it is great exercise.

Build a Little Free Library

These small libraries have been popping up in neighborhoods all over the country. This is a wonderful way to share your love of reading...and keep your house from getting cluttered with books you have read. Once you get started, it is likely that your library patrons will drop off their books as well. What a fun way to recycle! There is a wonderful website where you can get all the information you need to build your own Library. Look at littlefreelibrary.org for information on how to start your library, directions on building one, and how to install one. The site includes free downloads for different patterns. The possibilities are endless and depend on your carpentry skills and the age of your grandchild.

littlefreelibrary.org

Play Frisbee Golf

Get some small laundry baskets from a dollar store, and mark each one with a number... 1, 2, 3 and on depending how many stations you would like for your game.

You can play with Frisbees or tennis balls, whatever you have available. Take turns trying to get a frisbee into the basket from a marked distance. Young children should get a "handicap" and start closer to the goal. Keep score for each "hole" and remember: the person with the LOWEST score wins.

You can graduate from Frisbee Golf to Disc Golf, which is a modern game based on golf. It is designed to be played by people of all ages and is MUCH cheaper than golf. There are currently more than 100,000 members of the Professional Disc Golf Association! Who knew?

Disc Golf is a flying disc sport in which players throw a disc at a target; it is played using rules similar to golf. It is often played on a course of 9 or 18 holes. Players complete a hole by throwing a disc from a tee area toward a target, throwing again from the landing position of the disc until the target is reached. Usually, the number of throws a player uses to reach each target are tallied (often in relation to par), and players seek to complete each hole, and the course, in the lowest number of total throws.

The game is played in about 40 countries worldwide. Many city parks have courses already set up. Check it out in your area!

ON THE GO

Visit Your Grandchild's Home

Most of the items in this book assume that your grandchildren are coming to your house. But, don't forget the importance of a visit to their home.

Some things to include when you visit:
- Take a tour of their room. They will love to show you their treasures. Appreciate learning about their personality as reflected in their own surroundings.
- Tuck them in at night. Sing a silly song or read a book. There's nothing like saying good night to them in their own beds.
- Meet some of their friends.
- Attend a class with them….. ballet, sport, music. This will give you a great insight into their "normal" life.
- Take a walk around their neighborhood.

Attend a Seasonal Festival or Special Event

If you live near any of these top-rated festivals, plan to spend a day… or several.

- **New Orleans Jazz & Heritage Festival** in New Orleans, Louisiana This festival is a celebration of the music and culture of New Orleans. It is held during the last weekend of April and includes food, crafts, and many other attractions. There is a large kid's area so the kids participate in a genuine festival experience with music, puppeteers, and dance troupes.

- **ChocolateFest** in Burlington, Wisconsin This festival, held at the end of May, is 30 years old and features a carnival, Battle of the Bands, chocolate sculptures, chocolate eating, and chef demonstrations. This sounds like the perfect festival for chocolate lovers!
- **Lollapalooza** in Chicago, Illinois This annual summer music festival features popular artists from genres including rock, indie, electronic, hip-hoop, and more. There are dance and comedy performances, craft booths, and visual art. Kids 10 and under enter for free.
- **Austin City Limits** in Austin, Texas This three-day festival is held in Zilker Park. There are eight stages with over 400,000 attendees over the two weekends. The festival has become one of the biggest music festivals in the United States. Kids can enjoy a variety of interactive music and arts activities.
- **Green River Festival** in Greenfield, Massachusetts There are endless things for kids to do: Art Garden, frisbee golf, circus performances, a Mardi Gras parade, and a live music lineup geared for children.
- **Summerfest** in Milwaukee, Wisconsin This annual festival lasts from late June to early July and is promoted as the

World's Largest Music Festival. Kids can enjoy the Northwestern Mutual Children's Theater and Playzone which features a massive playground and rest area for families. There are magicians, dance groups, and jugglers.

- **National Cherry Festival** in Traverse City, Michigan There is something for everyone in this yearly festival. There are air shows, music, arts and crafts, wine tasting. You will also find fireworks and sand sculptures. And of course, there is the beauty of Lake Michigan.

- **The Laura Ingalls Wilder Pageant** in DeSmet, South Dakota This yearly pageant takes place over the month of July. There are theater performances, bus tours, visits to the Laura Ingalls Wilder Memorial Society and the Ingalls Homestead.

- **Oktoberfest Zinzinnati** in Cincinnati, Ohio Nearly 600,00 people attend this festival, so it must be good! There is plenty of schnitzel eating and polka dancing, but the favorite event is the Running of the Wieners. Daschunds race to be crowned the winning wicner. End of September NOTE: There is also a dachshund race at the Tulsa Oktoberfest in Tulsa, Oklahoma.

- **Sonoma County Harvest Fair** in Sonoma, California Though there is a lot of exceptional wine and beer, children can compete in the Grape Stomp. Early October

- **National Apple Harvest Festival** in Adams County, Pennsylvania Only a two-hour drive from Washington,

DC, or Baltimore, Maryland, this is accessible to many people. There are arts and crafts dealers, a petting zoo, antique cars, steam engine displays. Food includes apple dumplings, apple pizza, apple butter, and more. First two weekends in October

- **Cranberry Harvest Celebration** in Wareham, MA The centerpiece here is, of course, the cranberry. Helicopter rides are available as well the tamer pony rides, paddle boats, and wagon rides. Kids can put on waders and get knee-deep in the cranberry bogs. First part of October
- **Warrens Cranberry Festival** in Warrens, Wisconsin There are 850 arts and crafts booths and many contests such as Guess the Weight of the Largest Pumpkin. Great food is available: cranberry cream puffs and deep-fried cranberries on a stick. End of September
- **Albuquerque Balloon Fiesta** in Albuquerque, New Mexico This is advertised as the most photographed event in the world. There is a huge launch of all the balloons as well as the Balloon Glow, the Night Magic Glow, and the Special Shape Rodeo. There are fireworks at night... be sure to take a blanket and/or chairs. Beginning of October
- **Floresville Peanut Festival** in Floresville, TX This may not be a good idea if your grandchild has peanut allergies, but if you are peanut lovers, this could be fun. There are plenty of games, parades, and peanut treats. Mid October

- **Autumn at the Arboretum** in Dallas, Texas Featuring a Pumpkin Village, the Arboretum displays 4,500 chrysanthemums and 150,000 other blooming plants. There is a children's Adventure Garden. Late September until mid-November

- **Trailing of the Sheep Festival** in Hailey, Idaho The Sheep Parade features 1,500 sheep making their way down the middle of Main Street. There are traditional dancing and performances, fluff crafts, and art vendors. Mid October

- **New Hampshire Pumpkin Festival** in Laconia, New Hampshire Besides a great pancake breakfast, there is a Zombie Walk, horse-drawn hayrides, a climbing wall, bungee jumping, and other games and rides. Of course, you will also find pumpkin bowling, pumpkin carving, and a 34-foot tower of Jack-O-Lanterns. Mid October

- **West Coast Giant Pumpkin Regatta** in Tualitin, Oregon Another pumpkin festival with a different focus: costumed participants race their giant pumpkins across a lake. There are also magicians, clowns, food, etc. End of October

- **Wellfleet OysterFest** in Wellfleet, Massachusetts There is an Oyster Shuck-Off to determine who can shuck fastest. There are also musical performances, storytelling, arts and crafts, a fun run, and even a spelling bee. Mid October

- **North Carolina Pecan Harvest Festival** in Whiteville, NC Again, if your grandchild has any nut allergies, this would not be for you. Otherwise, there is a Pecan Run (5 K kid friendly run), art show, festival parade, cooking contest. The contest puts an emphasis on young cooks. End of October

- **Tecumseh Appleupmkin Festival** in Tecumseh, Michigan This is held in conjunction with the Kapnick Orchards Apple Festival. There are midway rides, carnival games, bouncy houses, crafts. mazes, and a scarecrow making tent. There is a not so scary Monster House for toddlers and young elementary school students. Mid October
- **Scarecrow Festival** in St. Charles, Illinois This October festival has over 100 scarecrows, so you will find your favorites to vote for. There is also live music, a petting zoo, and a make your own scarecrow tent.

If none of these events happen near you, you could plan a trip around your favorite. This list may also remind you of events closer to home.

Visit an Ethnic Neighborhood

There are so many possibilities, especially if you live in or near a big city.

- Go shopping in the 4500 block of North Clark Street in Chicago. This is a strip of mostly Korean owned shops that would be easy to miss. They offer startlingly inexpensive merchandise, around 70 per cent off typical retail prices.

- Old Salem in Winston-Salem, NC. This restored Moravian community has interesting architecture and lovely shops and bakeries.
- Chinatown. Everyone has heard of Chinatown in the San Francisco area, but there are also areas in New York, Chicago, Seattle, Boston, Los Angeles, and Philadelphia.
- Brighton Beach Brooklyn (Ukrainian and Russian culture)
- Greektown in Baltimore, Maryland
- Boston's North End (Italian)

A great way to enjoy some ethnic culture is to go to an ethnic restaurant. If you are looking for Czech food in Chicago, for example, go to Café Prague, Little Bohemian Restaurant or the Hletko favorite: Czech Plaza Restaurant in Berwyn, Il.

Visit an Airport

Though many large airports have programs in place that allow groups to tour, it is also possible that your small local airport will provide a guide to show you and your grandchild around. It would be very exciting to see some of the small, personal planes and hear about how the airport functions. Give them a call to see what is available.

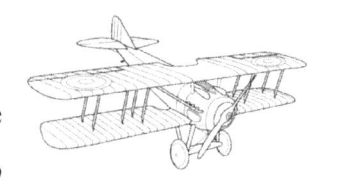

If airports don't interest you, think about touring a hospital, bank, local manufacturer, or a hotel. Call ahead to see what may be available and schedule a time.

Rent a Motel/Hotel Room; Swim for the Day

If any of the motel/hotels near you have indoor swimming pools, check on a day price. What fun it would be to check in, swim, have dinner, swim some more, and be home before bedtime. Buy some swim noodles at your local dollar store and be ready to play a couple of pool games.

Game 1: Red Light Green Light

This favorite lawn game can be played in a pool with slight changes. Use any red and green props to represent stop and go. That way, no one has to yell. All the players line up on one side of the pool. When the "light" is green, they rush as fast as possible toward to other side of the pool…the end line. When the "light" is red, they must not move. Besides being a fun competitive game, this is a great way to get young swimmers motivated to propel themselves through the water and also learning to tread water when they get deep enough that their feet no longer touch the bottom.

Game 2: Noodle Races in the Pool

This silly game is fun for kids and adults. This is another race from one side of the pool to another, but this time the participants must ride their noodles like horses. This may look easy, but racing this way is a good way to practice balance and strengthen arms for swimming.

Game 3: Invisibottle

This sounds a lot easier than it is! Fill an empty clear 2 liter plastic bottle and fill it with water. Have the players line up on the side of the pool with their backs to the pool. Toss the bottle into the pool; it will sink to the bottom. Once the players hear the bottle splash into the pool, they can turn around and dive or jump in to search for the bottle. Since the bottle will be nearly invisible, this is harder than you think! The first one to find the bottle wins.

NOTE: Remember the need for safety around a pool. This is incredibly important because in the 1-14 year age group, fatal drowning remains the second-leading cause of unintentional injury-related death behind motor vehicle crashes. Even a few minutes of inattention could lead to tragedy.

Attend a Special Event at a Zoo, Museum, or Garden

Museums, zoos, and other tourist destinations offer a variety of events through the year in order to increase their visits.

A few examples:

- **Brookgreen Gardens** in Murrells Inlet, SC, hosts Nights of a Thousand Lights around Christmas, but in 2018, they also had the Summer Lights Festival.

Sofie and Sydney at Brookgreen Gardens

- **Penguin Encounters:** In Chicago, Brookfield Zoo, Lincoln Park Zoo, and the Shedd Aquarium all have opportunities to interact with penguins.
- **Giraffe Encounters:** The Detroit Zoo, Chicago's Brookfield Zoo, the Cincinnati Zoo, the Boise Zoo, the Roger Williams Park Zoo, and Six Flags Discovery Kingdom all provide opportunities to interact with giraffes. Check their websites for details.
- **Museum overnights:** For an ultimate museum experience, see it at night without the crowds. In Chicago, Museum of Science and Industry, Field Museum, Adler Planetarium, Shedd Aquarium, and the Peggy Notebaert Nature Museum all offer special events. In New York, check out American Museum of Natural History. In San Francisco, check out the California Academy of Sciences. In Pittsburgh, look into the Carnegie Science Center. In Washington, DC, look into the National Museum of American History. If you are

in Britain, look at the Natural History Museum in London and The Hepworth Wakefield in West Yorkshire.

Museum staff will usually provide puzzles, games, activities. Some offer pizza parties. What a great birthday gift for your grandchild and a few friends.

- **Wonderland Express** at Chicago Botanic Garden

  This annual event features fabulous model trains, lots of indoor snow, and miniature Chicago landmarks. Ice sculptors set up outdoors with blocks of ice, chainsaws, and carving tools. Holiday wreaths made by Botanic Garden staff members are on sale in the Greenhouse Gallery.

- **Illumination at Morton Arboretum,** Lisle, Illinois

  Morton Arboretum's award-winning annual Illumination holiday light show is a one-mile walking tour through 50 acres of the arboretum, featuring innovative lights, music and projections.

- **Oglebay Winter Festival of Lights,** Wheeling, West Virginia

  The Oglebay Winter Festival of Lights features a six-mile drive, 90 lighted attractions and more than one million lights. One of the largest holiday light shows in the nation, the Winter Festival of Lights is energy-efficient, and showcases animated snowflakes and rainbow tunnels along with themed displays.

- **Hershey Park's Sweet Lights,** Hershey, Pennsylvania

At Hershey Park's annual Sweet Lights, families can drive through two miles of nearly 600 illuminated and animated displays—all from the comfort (and warmth) of your car.

- **Moody Gardens' Festival of Lights,** Galveston, Texas
This mile-long trail features more than one million lights and lighted scenes that illuminate the entire Moody Gardens property. There are phenomenal views of Galveston Bay.

Moody Gardens, Galveston, Texas

- **Garden Lights, Holiday Nights at Atlanta Botanical Garden,** Atlanta, Georgia
This annual extravaganza features thousands of lights throughout 30-acres of gardens including the Tunnel of Light, Radiant Rainforest and the Orchestral Orbs—all which showcase countless lights, fixtures and orbs.

- **Enchanted: Forest of Light at Descanso Gardens,** La Cañada Flintridge, California

The famous oak trees and botanical collections are the "stars of the show." Guests will see large-scale light displays and interactive installations—the famous Flower Power installation (a sea of illuminated tulips) is one of the show's biggest hits.

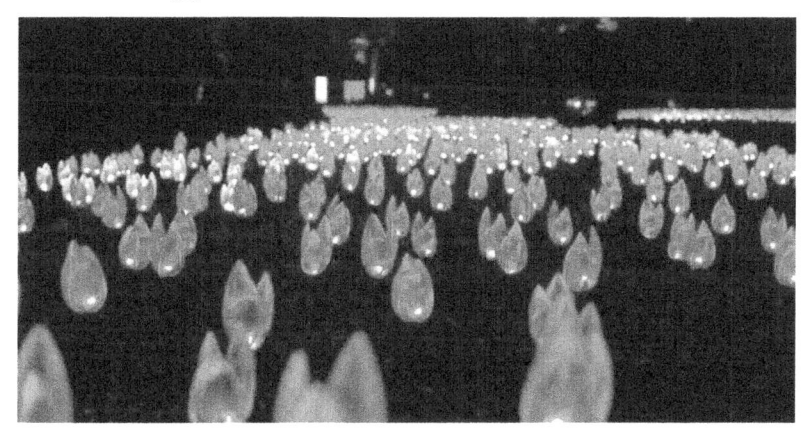

- **ZooLights at Smithsonian's National Zoo,** Washington, D.C.

  More than 500,000 environmentally-friendly LED lights greet guests at National Zoo's annual ZooLights show where visitors can enjoy various light-up animals throughout the zoo. NOTE: Lincoln Park Zoo in Chicago, Illinois, also hosts Zoolights.

- **Austin Trail of Lights,** Austin, Texas

  The Austin Trail of Lights is a community event that invites locals and tourists to the heart of Austin to experience everything and anything Austin-related—all in light form! From the city's delicious food and amazing music to its liveliness and family fun, the attraction features it all.

- **Las Vegas Motor Speedway,** Las Vegas, Nevada
This 2.5 mile circuit gives visitors the opportunity to stay in their cars and see more than 500 animated displays. The event is at the speedway but not on the track itself.
- **Denver Botanic Gardens,** Denver, Colorado
Visitors will see thousands of colorful lights among the Ponderosa pines, cottonwoods, and other native Western plants highlighted in the Gardens.

Go See the Synchronous Fireflies

(at Great Smoky Mountains National Park)

Frankie, a friend of Jana's, went to see the fireflies with her grandchildren and hasn't stopped talking about how wonderful it was.

Synchronous fireflies (Photinus carolinus) are one of at least 19 species of fireflies that live in Great Smoky Mountains National Park. They are the only species in America whose individuals can synchronize their flashing light patterns.

Fireflies (also called lightning bugs) are beetles. They take from one to two years to mature from larvae, but will live as adults for only about 21 days. While in the larval stage, the insects feed on snails and smaller insects. Once they transform into their adult form, they do not eat.

Their light patterns are part of their mating display. Each species of firefly has a characteristic flash pattern that helps its male and female individuals recognize each other. Most species produce a greenish-yellow light; one species has a bluish light. The males fly and flash and the usually stationary females respond with a flash. Peak flashing for synchronous fireflies in the park is normally within a two-week period in late May to mid-June. Due to the popularity of this event, there is a firefly shuttle from the

Sugarlands Visitor Center parking area to the Elkmont viewing area. These parking passes are distributed through a lottery on Recreation.gov-Firefly Event.

For more information about the fireflies and how to see them, visit https://nps.gov/grsm/learn/nature/fireflies.htm

Take a Boat Ride/Shelling Excursion

In the Low Country area of South Carolina, there are many opportunities to get out on the water even if you don't own a boat. Rover Boat Tours of Georgetown is one of the companies that offers shelling trips to North Island. The four hour cruise takes passengers through a bird-watcher's paradise, past South Carolina's oldest lighthouse and allows time to look for shells on a remote island. Obviously, there are also great opportunities in Florida, but wherever you live or visit, if you are near a river, lake, or ocean, look for a tour.

Audrey and Ellie enjoying a "sister moment" while they examine their shells.

Use Technology to Communicate With Grandchildren

Open any newspaper or magazine these days, and there will undoubtedly be an article about children, adults, and the use of cell phones instead of personal interaction.

Whether you live near or far away from your older grandchildren, you may find the best way to keep communication open is to turn to your computer or smartphone.

If you are not familiar with the basics for using these devices, there are classes at your local library that will get you up to speed. Another option, of course, is to check online for appropriate information or view a tutorial.

Nice overview of a smartphone:

https://www.bing.com/videos/search?q=basics+of+using+a+smartphone&&view=detail&mid=C1FA07CF71D5FBE5AEB9C1FA07CF71D5FBE5AEB9&&FORM=VRDGAR
or use the Tiny URL: https://tinyurl.com/yyf9yp91

For a slow paced, first-time user Smartphone overview by seniors for seniors try:

https://www.bing.com/videos/search?q=basics+of+using+a+smartphone&&view=detail&mid=F3F7E9BCFBF4248449BEF3F7E9BCFBF4248449BE&rvsmid=C1FA07CF71D5FBE5AEB9C1FA07CF71D5FBE5AEB9&FORM=VDQVAP
or use the Tiny URL: https://tinyurl.com/y439x9ny

-or-

just do a search for the particular thing you want to learn about.

Use Text Messaging

(The bubble icon is the APP for messaging/texting – generally just called texting)

NOTE: To keep things simple, the examples shown will be for an Apple iPhone screen.

Kids seldom want to talk on the phone these days; they much prefer to communicate via texting. In addition, texting can be incredibly helpful. For example, Lynn was recently "on call" to pick up her granddaughter from band practice after school. Natalie texted her when she was ready for pickup with specifics about where she would be waiting. Lynn responded and picked her up on time. Texting provided for a smooth, timely transaction.

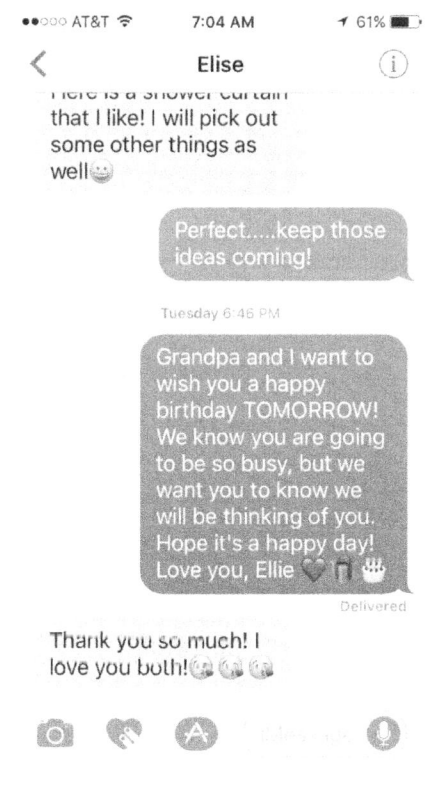

So, what if you don't know how to type much less how to "text?" Let voice recognition be your friend. You can now talk to your Smartphone and let it convert to text for you.

107

Every application that is "voice enabled" has a little microphone icon somewhere on the screen. When you click on that icon, you hear a beep telling you to talk now and then it displays the words you are speaking to it. in text form. When finished speaking click on "done" (if that shows up as a button) or just click on the line which shows the audio recording while you were talking.

Net result: You can send text messages back and forth to your grandkids without even trying to type.

Share Photos

The **photos** icon (circles of colors) allows you to view pictures you have taken with the camera of your iPhone. You can also share/send any pictures/videos with this APP). To share, click on the photo you want to share, then, click on the "share icon (box with an up arrow in it):

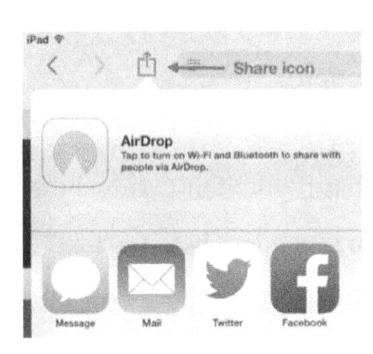

The share icon is a small square with an up arrow in the middle of it indicating your wish to send this to someone. Options include sending via the APPs for AirDrop (for apple users only) or Message, Mail, Twitter, or Facebook. Don't let the Airdrop or Twitter icon confuse you; just use one of your familiar APPs (Message, Mail, or Facebook.) Let your grandkids know you are "share savvy" in case they want to send something to only you.

WARNING: Keep in mind that pictures that are shared on social media are out there forever and can be used in negative ways. *The Wall Street Journal* (March 13, 2019, B1) has an interesting article with the headline *Think Before Sharing Your Baby's Photo*. The reporter Joanna Stern points out that parents (and by extension, grandparents) must take necessary precautions before sharing photos. Stacey Steinberg, a juvenile law attorney and professor at the University of Florida, said "Parents have to be clear that one day their children will come face-to-face with their disclosures." So, keep in mind your grandchild's right to privacy when you want to brag and show them off to your friends. You will also want to check with the parents about posting any pictures at all. If they allow you to post, they may request that there are no identifying dates or locations.

Use Video Conferencing (e.g. SKYPE)

A variety of other face-to-face technologies allow you to talk to and see your grandchildren whenever you want, and you can use them in a variety of ways. (Some examples are Facetime (Apple only), Skype (likes using the Outlook browser), Google Chat (prefers using Chrome browser).

You can witness first words, first steps, or first any things, new outfits, haircuts and art projects. You can sing songs together, or you can listen as they practice a presentation for you that they have to give at school the next day. Their parents can take their Smartphone along and you can watch your grandchild in a dance recital or at a basketball tournament.

Read A Book Together Long-Distance Style
Another way to stay in touch is to read together… even across the miles. You will need 2 copies of the same book. Send one to your distant grandchild and you keep the other. Then, at a prescribed time, make contact via Skype (or FaceTime). You can then read to your grandchild while you both follow along in your books. This will work for chapter books for the older children as well. Reading and discussing your books will forge a bond that will not be forgotten.

Directions for Using Videoconferencing
First download the APP you want to use (Apple Facetime is built in to your iPhone – it uses your regular apple ID and password)

For SKYPE or Google Hangout, you will need to first set up an account (provide an ID name like your email address) and create a password.

Once you have an account, instruct your videoconferencing APP to call someone by providing their phone # and click on "Call."

The person on the other end has to accept your call. If you both have your cameras on yourselves, you will have a video call. If one or both of you does not have a camera, it will just be a voice/speaker call.

It is a good idea to have someone who has experience with the process to help you the first time. It is a little hassle, but well worth it is see your grandchild's face light up when they see you and are able to talk face to face.

For more detail on how to get started go to

https://support.skype.com/en/faq/FA11098/how-do-i-get-started-with-skype

Use Old Fashioned Email

Email is perhaps the oldest and most common APP around. It allows people to communicate with a written record so they can go back and look at a message later or to pick up details they would never be able to remember from a just a verbal message. If your grandchild has an upcoming concert or sporting event, ask them to email you the details.

Use Facebook (Social Media)

Though Facebook has been around so long, the kids now call it the APP for old people, it is still a good APP for grandparents to see what their grandkids are up to and to organize some family events as covered in the earlier section on things to do in the Craft Room.

Lynn's great-nephew went to New Zealand for his semester abroad and she was able to enjoy photos he posted on Facebook that she likely would have never seen otherwise. She was thrilled to learn he had such a great opportunity and seemed to have enjoyed every minute of it.

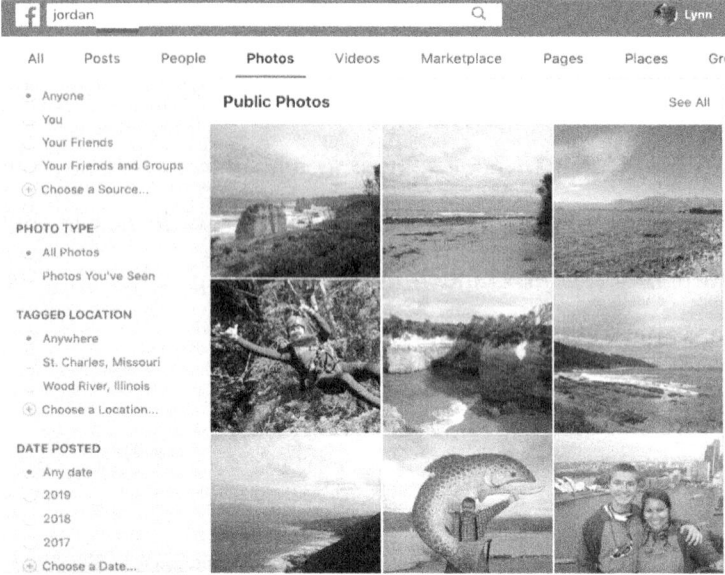

Although Facebook is a "public" APP you can restrict what you see and who sees what you post by "Friending" others who are using the APP. Some people are concerned about sharing personal information on Facebook and if you're one of them, you might prefer a different tool.

NOTE: When using the FB search bar, you will be presented with people who have the same or similar name and you can use their photo to help insure you have the right person. This is especially helpful to make sure you are "friending" your grandchildren and not someone else's grandchild. If not yet a friend, click on the "Add Friend" button and that person will receive a message inviting him/her to connect with you. They can either accept or reject. If accepted, you will then be connected and you can see each other's posts.

Notice the "Filter" window on the left side which allows you to choose between being public or restricting your communication to just **your** named friends.

Now when you go to the Facebook Homepage, you will see posts by anyone you have selected as a friend.

NOTE: This is how Lynn learned about her great-nephew in New Zealand. They had "friended" each other a while back but their communication had been dormant until she saw his post with photos in New Zealand. You can just view each other's posts or leave a comment about the post if you so desire.

To post something of interest you would like your friends to know about (like the arrival of a new grandchild) key in your message in the box that states "What's on your mind? You can also click on photo/video to attach a file to your post.

HINT: Look for the microphone to dictate your post into Facebook on your Smartphone.

Create a Family Only Facebook Group

Facebook has a feature to allow you to create a CLOSED group which means only members who are invited can see what is posted. It is a convenient way to avoid a lot of emailing about planning a family gathering or sharing photos with the family that you may not want to share with the public.

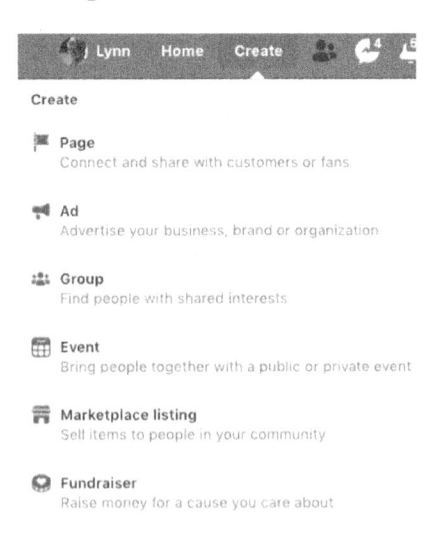

Assuming you already have a Facebook page, go to the top line and select "Create" – a pop down menu will appear – select "Group" – make sure your privacy setting says "closed group."

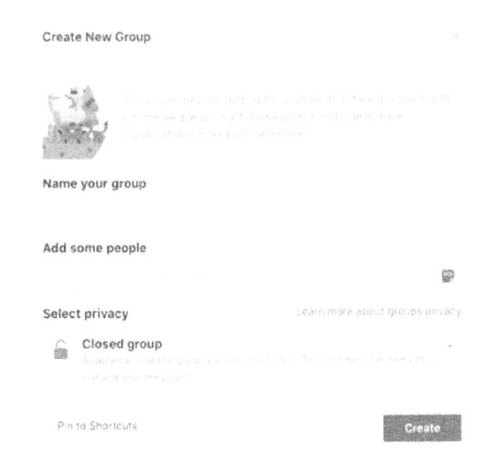

Next you will be presented with a screen to set up your group and invite some members (you can always add more later). Fill in the blanks and click "Create."

Now you can Add Photos

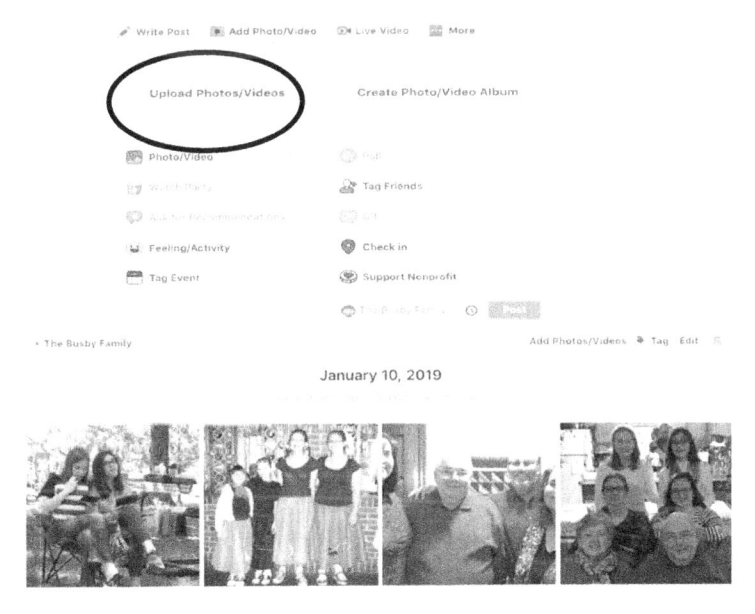

115

Add a Family Event on Facebook

Create an "Event" to help with planning and communication around an upcoming family gathering (NOTE: this assumes you have already created a "group" of your family members so the notice goes only to them.

This is a great way to organize and share photos from annual events like Mother's Day or Father's Day celebrations.

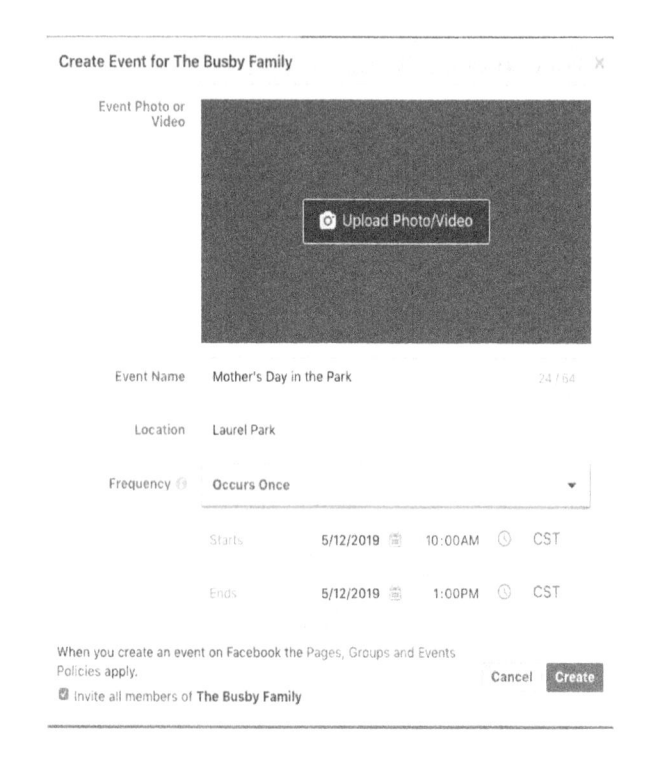

Use Facebook to Discover Events Around You

Let Facebook help you find events going on in your area that might make for a nice outing with the grandkids: (click on "Discover" on left hand menu)

Follow Your Grandchildren on Instagram

This is another APP that allows users to upload photos and videos to the (Instagram) service, which can be edited with various filters, and organized with tags and location information. It is photo oriented rather than text oriented – a way of showing others what you are up to right now.

An account's posts can be shared publicly or with pre-approved followers. Users can browse other users' content by tags and locations, and view trending content. Users can "like" photos, and follow other users to add their content to a feed.

Above Instagram photo from the National Geographic Instagram Account

Kids use it to "tag" their friends and just have fun with photos. You will be able to "like" or upload or comment on the pictures they post. Remember the social media warnings apply here, too.

Get To Know Internet Shortcuts the Kids Use

Get Creative With Emojis

Emojis are small pictures that represent something without using a lot of words. They were first used to try to express emotions (thus the origin of the name) Originally, a smiley face was used to express happy, but now there are emojis for a great number of things including sports, entertainment, food, music, transportation, etc.

There is a website showing the "standards" for emojis which can be found at
https://emojipedia.org/emojipedia/

Chances are good that your grandchildren will be tickled to see you use an emoji other than a happy face.

Try Using Some Texting Abbreviations

Texters like to use common abbreviations to save on typing and characters used in a limited message. Your grandchildren may be impressed if you know some of these. Below is a small sampling of the more common ones:

Abbreviation	What It Stands For
BRB	Be Right Back
ICYMI	In Case you missed it
IDK	I Don't Know
IMHO	In my Humble Opinion
IMO	In my Opinion
LOL	Laugh Out Loud
NRN	No Reply Necessary
OMG	Oh my God
PAL	Parents are Listening
PIR	Parent in Room
R	Are
ROFL	Rolling On Floor Laughing
THX	Thanks
TTYL	Talk to you Later
U	You
UR	Your
WTF	What The F*&^ (used all too commonly)

More info: Below is a good detailed guide on grandparents using the internet:
https://www.whoishostingthis.com/blog/2016/04/27/grandparents-internet/

Sometimes Things Won't Work As Planned

Keep in mind that some ideas just don't work out as planned. When the Hletkos were in Bar Harbour, Maine, in August, 2018, they planned a sunrise visit to Cadillac Mountain. This is the location of the first rays of sun in the United States and a popular tourist attraction. Everyone was up and in their cars by 4:15 a.m. Of course, the sun did rise that morning, BUT the fog obscured any view! Luckily, there was a breakfast cafe open that early, and everyone enjoyed blueberry pancakes.

Sun rise on Cadillac Mountain

About the Authors

Jana Dube Hletko

Jana Hletko and her pediatrician husband, Paul, have three married children and nine grandchildren. While Jana stayed home with their children when they were very young, she and her husband became interested in child car safety and helped get legislation passed in Michigan requiring the use of child car seats. She then worked for a community hospital in an education program to encourage seat belt and car seat use.

She is a creative educator, parent, and grandparent. She returned to teaching when they moved to South Carolina in 1989 and was one of the first 100 teachers in the United States to attain certification from the National Board of Professional Teaching Standards. In 1999-2000, she was the Georgetown County (SC) Teacher of the Year, and she was the South Carolina Journalism Teacher of the Year in 2005.

Her first book, *Cousins Camp* (updated to version *Cousins Camp 2.0* in 2019), explained how to plan and conduct a camp. The next book, *100 Plus Things To Do With Your Grandchildren,* provides ideas for lots of fun whenever you spend time with your grandchildren.

Lynn Zacny Busby

Lynn Busby and her husband Bob have four children between them and seven grandchildren as well as one great grandchild.

Lynn and Bob owned and operated an Apple Computer Dealership in the early days of personal computing (early 1980s). Both spent their careers in the computer business and also worked for large corporations including Toshiba, IBM, and MasterCard. With her intense computer background, she brings the skills needed to publish.

The Busbys are fortunate to have their children and grandchildren nearby. Over the years, they have spent countless hours in quality time with their grandchildren. They have babysat, vacationed together, and have been able to share birthdays and holidays. They have developed many family traditions that their grandchildren will always remember.

Lynn did all the technical work for Jana's first book and the revision as well. She was one of the friends who encouraged Jana to share what she had learned through her years of Cousins Camps. With her technical expertise, the book was published. Since the first book she and Jana have collaborated on two more books for grandparents.

Made in the USA
Monee, IL
06 December 2019